Also by Cees Nooteboom in English translation

FICTION

Philip and the Others

The Knight has Died

Rituals

A Song of Truth and Semblance

Mokusei!

In the Dutch Mountains

The Following Story

All Souls' Day

Lost Paradise

The Foxes Come at Night

NON-FICTION

Roads to Santiago: Detours and Riddles in the Land and History of Spain

Nomad's Hotel: Travels in Time and Space

Roads to Berlin: Detours and Riddles in the Lands and History of Germany

Zurburán: Selected Paintings 1625–1664

Letters to Poseidon

A Dark Premonition: Journeys to Hieronymous Bosch

POETRY

Self-Portrait of an Other

Light Everywhere

Monk's Eye

Cees Nooteboom

VENICE

THE LION, THE CITY AND THE WATER

With Photographs by Simone Sassen

Translated from the Dutch by
Laura Watkinson

MACLEHOSE PRESS
QUERCUS · LONDON

First published as *Venetië: De leeuw, de stad en het water* by De Bezige Bij, Amsterdam, in 2019
First published in Great Britain in 2020 by MacLehose Press

This paperback edition published in 2022 by

MacLehose Press
An imprint of Quercus Publishing Ltd
Carmelite House
50 Victoria Embankment
London EC4Y 0DZ

An Hachette UK company

This publication has been made possible with financial support from the Dutch Foundation for Literature

Nederlands letterenfonds
dutch foundation for literature

A CIP catalogue record for this book is available from the British Library.

ISBN (MMP) 978 1 52940 257 5
ISBN (Ebook) 978 1 52940 256 8

10 9 8 7 6 5 4 3 2 1

Designed and typeset in Haarlemmer by Libanus Press, Marlborough
Printed and bound in China

Papers used by Quercus Books are from well-managed forests and other responsible sources.

CONTENTS

The First Time

A FIRST TIME, THERE IS ALWAYS A FIRST TIME. IT IS 1964, a rickety old train from communist Yugoslavia, final destination: Venice. Beside me, a young woman, American. The long journey here has left its mark on us. Everything is new. We take the city as it comes. We have no expectations, except for those associated with the city's name, and so everything is good. It is all stored away in the secret tissue of the memory. The train, the city, the name of the young woman. We will lose touch, lead different lives, find each other again, much later on the other side of the world, tell each other our lives. More than fifty years after, that first day, in 1964, will find its way into a story, a story called "Gondolas". The city, and everything that had vanished in the meantime, will form the backdrop for that story.

In 1982, another city, another train. A friend has brought me to Victoria Station, in London. I am taking the Orient Express to Venice.

But the train is not there. Something somewhere is broken, and we do not travel over or under the sea, we fly across the world. Two days after that, the train leaves from Paris instead, a night train. I remember the stations at night, voices in the darkness, the rhythm that goes with trains, the invisible drummers that live somewhere underneath the carriages, loudspeakers announcing something in different languages.

I recognise the people who stood on the empty platform with me in London, but there are no spies among them, no great loves, no-one to go in a novel. The notes from this trip are in a different book, so I no longer have to carry them around. Years ago, I stored away the pink lamp from the luxury train that has stayed in that book, along with the people in evening dress, the extensive menus, the French of the waiters and their uniforms, as well as the sky-blue uniform of the man who ruled our compartment and is now wandering the cellars of memory. I can no longer keep him either, it may be the same life, but I have different things to do, I am on my way to the second of the first two times. This visit, I will share the city of water with no-one. It is 1982 in my then of now, the present tense of my sentences is embedded in a constant repetition, I will arrive and return here, the city will attract and repel me, I will have constantly different addresses in that place, I will keep on writing and reading about it, the city will become part of my life in a way that I will never be part of hers, I will drift through her history like a speck of dust, she will eat me up just as she has always devoured all her lovers and admirers, who over the course of the centuries have lain at her feet as if they themselves have imperceptibly turned to marble, a part of the air, of the water or the pavement, something you walk over, your eyes focused on the never-ending splendour of palaces and churches, briefly a participant in the story of the lion, the city and the water.

Slow Arrival

IN THE NOW OF THEN, IT IS FOGGY ON THE PO PLAIN. I am not in the mood for reading and so I look at the moving paintings outside – a false palm, an orange tree clipped bare, its foolish-looking fruits hanging like a reproach, but to whom? Weeping willows along a polluted brown river, trimmed cypresses, a cemetery with enormous mausoleums, as if boastful dead people live there, a clothesline with pink sheets on it, a capsized ship with a rotting keel, and then I am travelling across water, the whitish, mirroring, misty surface of the lagoon. I press my head to the cold window and see in the distance a grey hint of something that must be a city and which is now visible only as an intensification of nothingness, Venice.

In the station hall, the train has already fallen away from me, brown and painted it remains behind on the autumnal platform, I have once again become an ordinary passenger, someone who has arrived from Verona, a person with a suitcase, hurrying to the vaporetto. "The high bridges arched across the dim canals and there was a dark scent of moisture, moss and green decay, and the atmosphere of a centuries-old mysterious past, a past of intrigue and crime; dark figures skulked across the bridges, along the waterside, wrapped in cloaks, masked; two *bravi* seemed to want to slip the corpse of a white woman from a balcony . . . into the silent water! But they were only shades, merely phantoms of our own imagination."

That is not me, that was Couperus.[1] It is not a shade sitting opposite me, but a nun. She has a white face, long and narrow, and is reading a book about *educazione linguistica*. The water is black-grey, like oil, no sun is gleaming on it. We sail past walls that are closed, under attack, overgrown with moss and mould. I, too, see dark figures crossing the bridges. It is cold on the water, a penetrating damp chill coming in from the sea. I see someone inside a palazzo lighting two candles on a chandelier. All the other windows are closed behind flaking shutters and now the last one shuts too – a woman steps forward and makes that gesture that cannot be made in any other way: arms outstretched, she approaches the shutters, her figure silhouetted against the weak light, dimming herself into invisibility.

My hotel is just behind Piazza San Marco, from my room on the first floor I can see a few gondoliers still waiting for

1 Louis Marie Anne Couperus (1863–1923), Dutch author of poetry, novels and travel narratives.

tourists at this late hour, their black gondolas rocking a little in the death-coloured water. On the square I look for the spot where I stood when I first saw the Campanile and San Marco. It is long ago, but the moment remains unforgettable. The sun glanced off the square, onto all those rounded, feminine forms of arches and domes, the world turned ninety degrees and I felt dizzy. Here, people had done something that could not be done, on these few swampy pieces of ground they had come up with an antidote, a magic remedy for everything that was ugly in the world. A hundred times I had seen those pictures and yet I was not prepared, because it was perfect. That feeling of happiness has never left me, and I remember walking onto the square as if it were not permitted, out of the dark and narrow alleyways into that large, unprotected rectangle full of sun, with at one end that object, that impossible concoction of stone. I have been to Venice often enough since, and even though the lightning strike of the first time has not been repeated, there is still that mixture of delight and confusion, even now, with mists and flood planks. All the eyes that have ever seen this square – how much must they weigh?

I walk along Riva degli Schiavoni. If I went left, I would get lost in the labyrinth, but I do not want to go left, I want to keep walking along the veiled border between land and water, to the monument to the partisans, the large, fallen figure of a dead woman that the wavelets of the Bacino di San

Marco wash up against. It is cruel and sad, that monument. The darkness obscures the large, sombre body, which appears to move gently back and forth, the waves and the fog deceive me, it is as if her hair is fanned out with the motion of the water, as if the war is now, not then. She is so big because she wants something from our memory, a woman, much too large, who was shot dead and lies there in the sea until she, like all monuments, transforms from a bitter reminder of that one war and that one resistance into a sign that there is always war and always resistance. And yet, how easily a war is stripped of its blood if it is long enough ago. In the book I have with me, *The Imperial Age of Venice, 1380–1580*, the battles, the blood and the realms have been abstracted into hatching, arrows and erratic borders on the map of Italy, North Africa, Turkey, Cyprus and what is now Lebanon and the state of Israel, the arrows extending to Tana and Trebizond on the Black Sea, to Alexandria and Tripoli, and along the routes of those arrows the ships returned laden with the spoils of war and the merchandise that turned the city of water into a Byzantine treasury.

I take a boat to Giudecca. I have no reason to be there. Palladio's churches stand like closed marble fortresses, with passers-by walking around them like ghosts. Someone is at home – from behind the closed windows comes the muffled sound of a television. I go in and out of a few streets, want to reach the other side, but do not succeed. I can barely make out the lights of the city. This is what, for me, limbo might well look like, alleys with no exit, sudden bridges, corners, abandoned houses, sounds that belong to nothing, the call of a foghorn, footsteps moving away, faceless passers-by, their heads wrapped in shawls, a city full of spirits and the memory of spirits, Monteverdi, Proust, Wagner, Mann, Couperus, wandering in the constant proximity of that black, death-coated water, polished like a marble gravestone.

The next day I visit the Accademia. I have come for Veronese's so very secular *Last Supper*, but it is being restored, the room is closed off with a screen. The two restorers, a man and a woman, are sitting next to each other on a low bench and working on the tiles beneath the pink person and the green person, as I shall call them for the sake of simplicity. Using a stick with a white ball attached, they are rubbing something over an extremely small surface area, which is becoming lighter. The woman is wearing a shade of red that goes well with one of the figures. Now and then they lower their chemical sticks and discuss a colour or a direction, their gestures as theatrical as those of Veronese. I no longer remember if it was Baudelaire who compared museums to brothels, but what is certain is that there are always far more paintings that want something from you than the other way round. That is what makes the atmosphere in most museums so oppressive, all those square metres, painted with a purpose, attempting to woo you but with nothing to say, just hanging there to illustrate a period, to represent names, to perpetuate reputations. But today, as I wander away in disappointment from the hidden Veronese, I am in luck.

Something about a painting I have already passed calls me back, my brain has become snagged on something. I have never heard of the painter, Bonifacio de' Pitati. The work is called *The Apparition of the Eternal* (*Apparizione dell'Eterno*) and that is exactly what it looks like. Above the Campanile – which did in fact collapse in 1902, but the painter, who died centuries before, could not have known that – a dark cloud looms threateningly. The top of the tower cannot be seen, the cloud itself is layered and, arms outspread, wrapped in his own cloud-like cloak, which is even darker, an old man flies past, surrounded by heads and body parts – the ghost of a hand, a plump piece of arm flying upwards – belonging to that unappealing category of angels known as putti. A dove is escaping the darkness of the cloak and the lesser evil of the cloud, spreading a strange and penetrating light. My previous education has perfectly conditioned me to interpret images of this kind. These are the Father and the Holy Ghost and, unaccompanied by the Son, they are whizzing across the lagoon at great speed. San Marco is finely painted, all the rest is rather hazy, it requires some effort to realise that this church painted so long ago is in fact close to me now.

Human beings indicated by light brushstrokes occupy the large piazza. Some of them have raised their transparent, fly-winged arms, and yet this manifestation of the Eternal has not induced wide-spread terror, as would a shooting today. A few ships' sails have been touched by the dove's light, but none of those who are in the piazza becomes "nonymous", they have no faces and therefore no names, no characters, they just represent a crowd. With difficulty, the hint of a dog frees itself from the painted pavement, a patch that depicts a dog among other patches that are also material and yet depict nothing, no nouns, just the nuances of colour and stone, added touches. Someone is carrying a barrel or a heavy bundle of wood and so they are walking with a stoop, many people are grouped around one, but it is not clear why, goods of some kind hang from the canopy of a stall, elongated hares, cloths, bunches of lavender, only the painter knew what. The Apparition pushes their tiny shadows in his direction of flight, the domes of San Marco are narrowed, bulging, they did not turn out well during the glass-blowing, too high and too thin.

Once again I peer, as if I myself might stand among them, at those strange rows of human beings, earlier Venetians. They are lined up as if at a British bus stop, but without the stop itself, the waiting they have to do appears to begin at some mysterious and insignificant spot, it is a place I would like to find on that piazza later, indicated by a formula that could only be read by me, so that I, and no-one else, would see the Eternal, who there, and only there, in the guise of an old man chasing a dove, would fly past as if he might still catch up with Icarus.

A Dream of Power and Money

A DIFFERENT THEN, A DIFFERENT NOW. TIME WEIGHS nothing here. Today I am thinking about water. Everything is an exercise in repetition, the city needs to be conquered over and over. Palude del Monte, Bacino di Chioggia, Canale di Malamocco, Valle Palezza, how wonderful it would be to approach Venice again for the first time, but surreptitiously, sailing up to the labyrinth through that other labyrinth of the marshes, between the water creatures, in the early-morning fog of a January day like today, with nothing but the sound of the birds and the splashing of the oars, the brackish water quiet and gleaming, the vision in the distance still veiled, the city wrapped in its own mystery. Palude della Rosa, Coa della Latte, Canale Carbonera, on the big map of the lagoon the waterways seem to be drawn like waving seaweed, like plants with bent, moving tentacles, but they are ways through the water, ways you have to know just as a fish knows its way, channels in water that becomes land again at low tide, wetland with sucking mud, the hunting grounds of the redshank and the sandpiper on their eternal search for worms and small shells in their home of water and sand. They were once the first inhabitants, and if that city one day sinks, like an infinitely slow *Titanic*, back into the soft ground upon which it now appears to float, they will perhaps be the last, as if between those two moments the world has dreamed something that is impossible, a dream of palaces and churches, of power and money, of dominion and decline, a paradise of beauty that had been driven out of itself because the world could not bear such a great wonder.

As is known, we cannot truly imagine eternity. What, to my mind, appears to come closest is something like the number one thousand, probably because of the rounded emptiness of those three zeros. A city that has existed for more than a thousand years is a tangible form of eternity. I think this must be why most people walk around here feeling a little ill at ease, lost among all those layers of past time, which in this city are at once part of the present. In Venice, anachronism is the essence of things themselves, in a church from the thirteenth century you look at a grave from the fifteenth century and an altar from the eighteenth century, what your eyes see is what the now-defunct eyes of millions of others have seen, though there is certainly no tragedy in that here, because as you look they go on talking, you are in the constant company of the living and the dead, taking part in a conversation that is already centuries old. Proust, Ruskin, Rilke, Byron, Pound, Goethe, McCarthy, Morand, Brodsky, Montaigne, Casanova, Goldoni, Da Ponte, James, Montale, just like the water in the canals, their words flow around you, and just as the sunlight shatters the waves behind the gondolas into a thousand small sparks, in all those conversations, letters, sketches, poems, one single word echoes and sparkles: Venice, always the same, always different. Paul Morand named his book about the city *Venises* for good reason, and even that is not in fact sufficient. A superlative form of the plural should exist just for this island.

I did not come across water, I came from the sky, from one city of water to the other. A person who behaves like a bird, that can never end well. Then by taxi across the bridge that should never have existed, with a driver who is in a tearing hurry, a person who behaves like a hunting dog, I can feel that this is not fitting, not here. But I have armed myself, I am armoured with the past. In my luggage I have the 1906 Baedeker and the 1954 Touring Club Italiano guide. The railway station is still where it should be, I am not going to wonder how many people have arrived here by train since 1906. "Gondeln mit einem Ruderer 1-2 fr., nachts 30 c. mehr, mit zwei Ruderern das doppelte, Gepäck jedes kleinere Stück 5 c. Gondeln sind stets ausreichend vorhanden, ausserdem bis gegen Mitternacht die Stadtdampfer (Koffer und Fahrräder nicht zugelassen, Handgepäck frei). Bahnhof S. Marco 25 min. Fahrpreis 10 c. Pensionen, Riva degli Schiavoni 4133, deutsch, Zimmer von 2½ fr. an. Möblierte Zimmer (auch für kurze Zeit), Frau Schmütz-Monti, Sottoportico Calle dei Preti 1263. Hotel: H. Royal Danieli, nahe dem Dogenpalast, mit Aufzug, 220 Z. von 5 fr. an mit Zentralheizung." In 1954, a trip by gondola from the Stazione Ferroviaria to the *alberghi del centro* for two people with a maximum of four suitcases already cost fifteen hundred lire, the amounts later rocketing to the astronomical figures of space travel. Louis Couperus travelled to Venice at the beginning of that century with ten suitcases and was surrounded by a cloud of porters, but progress has turned us into our own servants, and so I haul my two stubborn suitcases between the legs of the crowd and onto the vaporetto for a sum that a family could have lived on for a week back in the days of Rilke and Mann. Half an hour later, I have taken up residence on the alpine peak of four marble staircases in an alleyway where you have to keep your elbows tucked in, but from six narrow windows I have a view of the intersection of two canals, which as an Amsterdammer I would call *grachten.* As I open one of those windows, a gondola sails by with eight frozen Japanese girls and a gondolier singing "O sole mio". I am in Venice.

Quarter, half-hour, hour, the bronze voices of time that you no longer hear in other cities, here they assail you in alleyways and on bridges, as if it is time itself that is pursuing you to tell you which part of him (in Dutch, time is masculine – why is that?) has just been lopped off. You are lost in the labyrinth, you are looking for Santa Maria dei Miracoli, which Ezra Pound called a "jewel box", you know you are close, but the name of the alley you find yourself in is not on your oh-so-extensive map, a bell is ringing, but you do not know if it is the bell of the church you are looking for, and then another rings, and another, and that one is not talking about time now, it is shouting something about death, sombre, heavy chimes, or about a marriage, or a high Mass, and then the bells are galloping against one another as if taking part in a race. At twelve midday, the Angelus sounds. I remember the Latin words from my schooldays: *Angelus Domini nuntiavit Mariae*, the Angel of the Lord declared unto Mary, and at the same time you see them in front of you, all those Annunciations in the Accademia, in the Ca d'Oro, in the churches, by Lorenzo Veneziano, and by the Bellinis, Byzantine and Gothic, over and over the winged man and the virgin, you have seen them so often that you are no longer surprised a man has wings, any more than you are surprised by the other dream figures, crowned lions, unicorns, people flying through the air, griffins, dragons, they just happen to live here. You are the one who is lost in the realm of the dream, the fable, the fairy tale, and if you have any sense, then you will let yourself be lost. You were looking for something, a palazzo, the house of a poet, but you have lost your way, you turn down an alleyway that ends in a wall, or onto a canal without a bridge, and suddenly you realise that this is what it is all about, that now you are seeing things you would not otherwise see. You stand still, and what you hear is footsteps, the forgotten noise that belongs to an age without cars, which has sounded here without interruption for all these centuries. Shuffling, angry, hurried, slow, ambling steps, an orchestra with instruments made of leather, rubber, wood, sandals, high heels, boots, trainers, but always a human rhythm, swelling in the hours of light, and then, when it becomes dark, gradually diminishing until all you can hear is *soli*, and finally the lonely aria of your own feet reverberating in the dark and narrow alleyway, on the marble steps, and then only silence, until the city wants to say something for the last time: that midnight comes in fairy tales too.

From my high windows I can hear, within the all-embracing silence, the Marangona, the big bell of the Campanile ringing again, muffled, heavy, commanding strokes. The city on the water is closing, this is the end of all the stories, go to sleep. No more movement on the still water below, no voices, no footsteps. The doge is sleeping, Tintoretto is sleeping, Monteverdi is sleeping, Rilke is sleeping, Goethe is sleeping, the lions, dragons, basilisks, the statues of saints and heroes, all are sleeping, until the first boats with fish and fresh vegetables come in and the symphony of the hundred thousand feet begins again.

Zinc-coloured light, the painter does not yet know quite what to do with this day, leave it as is, throw in more copper, with a greenish tinge, accentuate the grey, or allow more light to flow over everything. Weather for bats, when it starts to rain everyone puts up their umbrella, transforming into bats themselves. Five minutes later, the sun is shining again, the wind blows across Riva degli Schiavoni, the water is as agitated as a nervous actress, I can smell the sea at my feet, because I have sat down on a small wooden staircase that extends some way into the water. Petrarch lived here, as I just read behind me, *l'illustre messer Francesco Petrarca essendogli compagno nell'incantevole soggiorno l'amico Giovanni Boccaccio*, and now I want to see what they saw when they stood in front of the house, these two masters with their contemplative eyes. The tip at the end of the *sestiere* of Dorsoduro, where two Atlases must now carry the golden globe on the tower of the Dogana, but that was not there back then. It used to be known as Punta del sale, because of the many salt warehouses on the Zattere. And right opposite, on the small island where the classical violence of San Giorgio Maggiore now stands, was a Benedictine abbey, which, if Petrarch and Boccaccio were standing beside me, would have mysteriously disappeared. How would I explain Palladio to them? Nostalgia for the pure lines of pre-Christian Rome that built these enormous, triumphant temples over their humble, probably pre-Roman, probably brick abbey from 982, just as that same pagan nostalgia constructed the equally proud Redentore a few hundred metres further along on Giudecca, and the Salute just past the Dogana by the Canal Grande. The two masters would recognise only San Marco, at least its shape, the rest would be a vision, something that in a mysterious way simultaneously looks like a conceivable past and an unimaginable future. But these are once again the dreams of anachronism, and this time they are forbidden dreams, because as I sit there musing, I see a small police boat sail around me, turn, come back, manoeuvring as only Venetians can who are born on the water. The carabiniere sticks out his head and says that I may not sit there: I am four metres too far out from the coast on my coconut matting, this is Zona Militare. Obediently, I stand up, I can hardly explain that I am having a conversation with Petrarch and Boccaccio, and the naval power of La Serenissima is not a force to be trifled with – just go and ask all the coasts of this sea!

It is inevitable. You have been wandering around the Accademia all day long, you have seen a square kilometre of painted canvas, it is the fourth, the sixth, or the eighth day and you feel as if you have swum against a mighty current

of gods, kings, prophets, martyrs, monks, maidens, monsters, that you have been travelling constantly with Ovid, Hesiod, the Old and the New Testaments, that the Lives of the Saints, the Christian and pagan iconography are pursuing you, Catherine's wheel, Sebastian's arrows, Hermes' winged sandals, Mars' helmet and the stone, golden, porphyry, marble, ivory lions are all out to get you. Frescos, tapestries, funerary monuments, everything is laden with meaning, refers to real or imaginary events, hordes of sea gods, putti, popes, sultans, condottieri, admirals, all of whom want your attention. They flit across the ceilings, looking at you with their painted, woven, drawn, sculpted eyes. Sometimes you see the same saint several times in one day, in a Gothic, Byzantine, Baroque or classical guise, for myths are powerful and the heroes adapt, Renaissance or Rococo, they do not care, as long as you look, as long as their essence remains intact. Once they were employed to express the power of their masters at a time when everyone knew what they represented, Virtue, Death or Dawn, War, Revelation, Freedom, they played their allotted roles in the allegories, they commemorated confessors and church fathers, generals and bankers, now other hordes march past, tourists who no longer understand their visual language, who no longer know what they mean or meant, only their beauty has remained, the genius of the master who made them, and they stand there, a nation of stone guests, waving from the façades of churches, leaning forward from the *trompe l'œils* of the palazzi, the children of Tiepolo and Fumiani skimming through the air, and again Saint Julian is beheaded, again the Madonna cradles her child, again Perseus fights the Medusa and Alexander speaks to Diogenes. The traveller retreats from all this violence, for a moment he wants no more of it, to sit on a stone bench by the water's edge, to watch a Slavonian grebe seeking prey in the brackish green, to look at the movement of the water itself, to pinch himself to make sure he is not sculpted or painted. Could it be, he thinks, that there are more Madonnas in Venice than living women? Does anyone know how many Venetians are painted, sculpted, carved in ivory, embossed in silver? And just imagine, he thinks, but this is only because he is so tired, that one day they all rebelled at once, abandoning their frames, niches, predellas, pedestals, tapestries, eaves, chasing the Japanese, the Americans, the Germans out of their gondolas, occupying the restaurants and, with their swords and shields, their purple cloaks and crowns, their tridents and wings, finally demanding their reward for ten centuries of faithful service?

A day of small things. Sitting on the foredeck of the vaporetto, in spite of the cold and wind, lashed by the rain, hopping from the jetty onto the deck and from the deck onto the jetty, wishing you were transported in this fashion every day, always surrounded by that moving element of water, the promise of travel. Once, in 1177, the powerful Venetians forced Barbarossa to kiss the foot of Pope Alexander III, here, in the entrance of San Marco, and then to help His Holiness into the stirrups of the papal mule, outside on the piazza. As a sign of gratitude, the Pope gave the doge a ring with which he could marry the sea every year on Ascension Day: "We marry you, the sea, as a sign of our true and perpetual dominion." The sea subsequently cheated on her spouse, who was always new but always the same, multiple times, but in one respect she remained faithful: every morning still there is a silver treasure laid out on the stone tables of the fish market, *orata* and *spigola*, *capone* and *sostiola*, and all those other colours, the *seppia* smeared with ink as if the writer has been trying to work things out, the still-alive and squirming *anguilla*, red with blood from the gouges of the cleaver, the crab still looking for life with its eight legs, the living stones of mussels, oysters, cockles – every medieval person would recognise them, just as they would likewise recognise the Pescheria, which has been here on the Canal Grande by the Rialto, next to San Giacomo, the oldest church in Venice, for more than a thousand years.

I entered beneath the oversized clock with the one hand and the twenty-four mighty Roman numerals, past the five slender columns with their Corinthian capitals, which have been looking out over fish and vegetables since 900. If I have understood my guides correctly, everything inside here has been rebuilt and converted, but now is not the moment to think about art history. An elderly priest in a green chasuble is blessing his parishioners and is about to say something else. The little church is full, looks like a front room where the residents have kept their coats on. They are among their own, they know one another, they seem to know that people have prayed in this place for fifteen hundred years, as if they themselves had stood at the deathbed of the Roman gods, just as they also heard from outside the peculiar noise of the Reformation, the French Revolution, the rattling of an iron curtain and the cries from the Sportpalast. Nothing here had changed in the meantime. Someone who had later embraced a carthorse in Turin apparently declared that God was dead, but they had continued to speak to him in the same words they had always used to speak to him, and now the old man shuffled to the altar of Saint Anthony Abbot, held up a relic of the saint, a bone or a piece of his cowl behind glass, I could not quite make it out. The priest asks if the great desert saint will aid us in our *debolezza*. When I look up that word later, just to make sure, I see that it means “weakness”, a description that is not inappropriate. Afterwards, the men talk for a while beneath the six eternal lamps with oil flames glowing behind their red glass. The priest leaves, wrapped in a plastic jacket, which looks far too thin, over his cassock, and everyone shakes hands. I glance over at the confessional.

A skimpy little purple curtain hangs in front of it, those confessing have no chance to hide, anyone whispering their sins here might as well broadcast them out loud. The walls still whisper messages about the guild of the oil pourers (*travasadori d'olio*), the grain-sieve makers and the porters, about the doge who, through the centuries, came here every Thursday before Easter to worship the saint, but I have an appointment with the greatest of all Venetian painters, at the Scuola di San Giorgio degli Schiavoni: Vittore Carpaccio. He has his own room in the Accademia, in which you become trapped in his universe when he tells the legend of Saint Ursula on all four walls, a series of paintings about which you should write a book. Here in the Scuola the splendour is no less, but today I have returned to this small and intimate space to see one painting, the vision of the greatest saint among writers and the greatest writer among saints, Augustine of Hippo. Maybe it is because the painting depicts a writer's room, one that I would like to move into at once. Fine, I cannot lay claim to the mitre on the altar, the staff, the Christ with cross and flag, but the perfect light, the open books, the music score, the shell, apparently a *Cypraea tigris*, the beautiful bound folders on the left wall, which may contain manuscripts, the revolving bookcase, the intriguing letter lying somewhere in the middle of the floor, and the small woolly dog with his two legs sticking straight out, his nose in the air and those two bright, cherry-black eyes, no, someone who cannot write here should not attempt it anywhere. The saint himself has been caught at the most mysterious of all moments, the moment of inspiration. He is holding his pen in the air, light is streaming in, he hears the words taking form and knows almost how he will write them down; a second later, when Carpaccio has left, he dips his pen into the cuttlefish ink and writes the sentence that is now preserved in every library in the world in one of his books.

End. A last day, which in another year will become a first, as between Venice and Venice a lot may be forgotten. I am going to visit the dead. From Fondamente Nove, I take the vaporetto that sails to the island of the dead, San Michele, and then on to Murano. In a wonderful novella by Alejo Carpentier, *Concierto barroco*, there is a scene in which Handel and Vivaldi, the red-haired Venetian priest, following a wild carnival night of music and wine, go for breakfast with some other people on the island of the dead. They drink and eat, "while Vivaldi, chewing on a piece of boar's head marinated in vinegar, oregano and red pepper, walked away a few steps and stopped at a nearby grave, which he had been looking at for quite some time, as it was adorned with a name unheard of in those parts. 'IGOR STRAVINSKY,' he said, spelling it out. 'That's right,' said Handel, in turn spelling out the letters, 'he wanted to be buried in this cemetery.' 'A decent musician,' Antonio said, 'but sometimes very old-fashioned in his approach. He was inspired by the usual themes: Apollo, Orpheus, Persephone . . . how much longer?' 'I know his *Oedipus Rex*,' said Handel. 'There are those who think the end of the first act (*Gloria, gloria, gloria Oedipus uxor!*) is reminiscent of my music.' 'But . . . whatever possessed him to write a profane cantata to a Latin text?' asked Antonio. 'His *Canticum Sacrum* was performed too, at San Marco,' Georg Friedrich said. 'It contains melismas in a medieval style we have long since abandoned.' 'Yes, those so-called avant-garde masters try so terribly hard to figure out how the composers of the past did it . . . sometimes they even try to update their style. We are more modern. I could not care less what the operas or concerts of a hundred years ago were like. I follow my own path, according to my ability and insight, and that is that.' 'I think exactly the same,' said Handel, '. . . although of course one should not ignore the fact that —' 'Piffle,' said Filomeno, knocking back the bottle of wine he had just uncorked. And the four of them reached once again into the baskets from the Ospedale della Pietà, baskets that, like the mythological horn of plenty, never became empty. But when it was time for the quince jelly and the convent pastries, the last morning clouds parted and the sun fell directly on the tombstones, which now lay as brilliant spots of white under the deep green of the cypresses. The bright light made the Russian name, so close to them, catch their eyes once more."

It is almost closing time when I arrive at the cemetery. I walk past the gatekeeper, get a map of death with the lodgings of Stravinsky, Diaghilev, Ezra Pound and the more recently added Joseph Brodsky. It is unseemly; everyone is sleeping and I am nearly in something like a hurry. I walk past the graves of children, marble constructions for souls who lived just a single day and portraits of boys whose invisible footballs can still be seen in their eyes, across the dividing line between the Militari del Mare and those della Terra, as if these distinctions still count where they are now, and soon come to the Protestant section, truncated columns, mossy pyramids, the nineteenth-century grammar of death, palms, cypresses, most of the graves already dead themselves, their inscriptions illegible, Danes, Germans, consuls, nobility, and among all that the two slabs of Olga Rudge and Ezra Pound, within a low, heart-shaped enclosure of plants, and nearby a small hill of almost sand-coloured soil with a few bunches of wilted, withered flowers and a thin and simple cross of white wood with pebbles on its arms: Joseph Brodsky. Behind the wall, in the Reparto Greco, Igor and Vera Stravinsky lie among Russian princes and Greek poets. Handel and Vivaldi have just departed, but they left their flowers, a pink rose and a blue iris on each of the two graves, laid in a cross. I think about how many years ago it is that, in New York, I asked Vera Stravinsky if, towards the end of his life, when he was over eighty, Stravinsky did not

find the repeated travelling to Venice tiring, and with that glorious Russian accent she replied: "Ach, you don't understand! Stravinsky, he lovved the flyink!"

A mechanical voice from the realm of the dead rings out over the island, a herald as polyglottal as the Pope. In German, English, Russian, Japanese, we are requested to leave the dead in peace, the gates are closing. Run, *ragazzi*, run, call the gravediggers, whose trained ears have already heard the vaporetto coming, and we all run together to the dock, as if someone were chasing us with a scythe. When we are out on the open water, I see Murano on one side, Venice on the other. The orange lights that indicate the navigation channel have come on, the two islands, the big one and the small one, float on the dark water like ghosts, and then, from behind a black cloud, comes the copper clash of sunset, casting the city in front of me in an apocalyptic glow for ten seconds, as if that dream down below has now lasted long enough.

The Shattered Labyrinth

I HAVE BOUGHT AN ALMOST IMMEASURABLE MAP OF the lagoon of Venice in an attempt to restore the city to her correct proportions. A curious exercise. I know that I will arrive there tomorrow from the air, and that this time I will approach the city itself, which I have visited so often before, from across the water. On the map, the ratio of water to city is perhaps a thousand to one, in the endless blue the city has become a little town, a small clenched fist on an outspread sheet, so that it seems as if all that emptiness, in a moment of fury, once brought forth the city that would later rule over it. The Mexican writer Valeria Luiselli sees my fist as a broken kneecap, and when I look closely I see that she is right. From the height of Google Earth, this becomes even more evident, the Canal Grande is the fracture in the knee; the grainy, shattered labyrinth around it is the bone of the city in which tomorrow I will once again become lost, just as everyone who comes from outside must get lost there; it is the only way to get to know her.

I have had several addresses here, sometimes in old hotels, usually down dark and narrow alleyways, parts of a palace that never looked like a palace, dilapidated stairwells, small rooms with what just about passes for a window, looking out onto a house at the back, where no-one seemed to live, and yet outside on a rickety line two frozen pairs of panties hung in the still, freezing coldness. The occasional view of the water of an unknown side canal where, every day at the same time, a boat laden with fruit and vegetables came by. This time it is not winter, but September, and any dream of an empty city evaporates upon arrival: Venice belongs to the entire world, and the whole world has come to visit, if there is a Proust or a Thomas Mann, a Brodsky or a Hippolyte Taine among them, they cannot be seen. It is the advancing armies that are on the move during this season, the Chinese army, the Japanese army, the Russian army. Anyone who wants to find his own Venice will have to be stubborn and determined, clad in invisible armour, and humbly remember that for all those other people he too is simply another person who is getting under their feet and annoyingly standing pressed up against them in the central section of the vaporetto without anything to hold on to.

But we are not yet at that point. I have only just arrived and have already mixed three of the four elements into my journey: I came through the sky and walked across the earth to the glinting water I am now facing, on a jetty, as I wait for a taxi. I do not dare to take on the fourth element, fire, even though the sunlight is flaming on the swaying water. After all, there are limits to the art of description these days, related to the new reader's patience. Before my departure, I bought a book written by Hippolyte Taine in 1858, and the passages I had marked were about the sparkling in the movement of the water, and that is also a lesson in humility, because in his description the water truly sparkles. Now that I am standing here, I see how difficult it is to do what the nineteenth century was still able to do without any shame: to describe, in minute detail, our impressions of what can be seen.

The taxi puts a stop to my reflections, slicing open the water of the wide lagoon, flying past the geometrical lines of the mooring posts across what must be Canale di Tessera and pouncing upon the city. I see the silhouettes of the familiar towers, for a second I have the feeling that I am coming home, we shoot by Murano and beneath San Michele, the island of the dead, and sail in past the Arsenale, slowing along the brick walls of the high quay and then diagonally across Canale di San Marco to the small island of San Giorgio, where I will be living this time. It is not my fault that the bells of the mammoth San Giorgio start to ring: it is six in the evening, time for the Angelus. Across the water I can now hear the bells of San Marco and the Redentore too. In a crossfire of sound, I stand on the large open piazza in front of the church and see a man on his knees with a steel brush, which is far too small, trying to scrub away, centimetre by centimetre, the seaweed that has grown on the steps just below the water's surface, a Sisyphean task that seems to have more to do with eternity than the world from which I arrived today.

An hour later, after taking my suitcase to my monastery room, I walk into the enormous church, which is still open. It is the kind of space in which you instinctively seek out the side walls: the emptiness in the middle is dangerous. I do not know whether people can pray here. There is no trace of the intimacy of Romanesque churches: this is a space station for the departure to Mars, a different, classical and martial

god rules here in the house that Palladio devised for him. Even the large expanses of the Tintorettos, which are scarcely visible in the semi-darkness, are subsumed in the mathematical network of unrelenting lines. I know that behind the mighty high altar there are supposed to be magnificent Flemish choirstalls, but as I am about to walk towards them I am stopped in my tracks by the sound of voices, a soft yet whining murmur of old men.

This was once a Benedictine monastery. Later, after the monks were ousted, everything fell into a state of disrepair. Now there is a foundation based on the island, where I am permitted to live for the next few days, but the monks have returned to their shrunken monastery. They occupy only four of the many choir stalls, I have positioned myself in the growing darkness so that I can see them during their Vespers. Their voices, with that Gregorian humming, drown within the dimensions of the building, the contrast between classical pomp and helplessly whispered prayers is not without pathos; there is an atmosphere of irrevocable farewell, and when I tiptoe out of the space station, I hear behind me the echo, growing weaker and weaker, of an age that is gone for good. Outside, I see the lights of the piazza across the water and the boats sailing from the Schiavoni to Giudecca. I am back.

What would it be like to live here all the time? I remember that question occupying me, almost twenty-five years ago now, when I lived for a while in the walled city of Berlin. You could leave, but it was not easy. As time went by you became accustomed to it, and yet the feeling of being locked in was always present somewhere in the background. The situation is not comparable, the wall around Venice is made not of stone but of water, when I step outside in the morning my gaze is focused not on concrete and bricks but on a wide open space, and yet, in a mysterious way, the absence of buses, cars and traffic lights, in itself pleasant, also serves as an invisible separation from the rest of the world, and I notice that I have a feeling of freedom as I stand on the Fondamente Nove and wait for the vaporetto to Torcello. Let there be no misunderstanding, I am happy in Venice, but it is happiness with an aftertaste, perhaps because of the accumulated past, the excess of beauty, because it is too much happiness, the tension of the labyrinth which, sometimes several times a day, leads you into some closed courtyard, up to a brick wall, or to water without a bridge, so that what should open up is suddenly closed and you have to turn around, go back to where you came from. Just for a moment the city was holding you prisoner, just for a moment you were the fly in the web, the prisoner of Borges, obstructed by a net of a thousand churches and palazzi, squeezed into narrow and dark alleyways, and now, abruptly, that is over, you are standing in the light of the waterfront, you see the ships moving criss-cross through all that light and behind them the miniature of Murano, which lies glittering in the September glow. Closer, just across the water, is San Michele, the island of the dead, with its tall cypresses as guards, but that is not sad, because you know that Brodsky, Stravinsky and Diaghilev are out there, lying around Pound's grave and humming Russian songs until the end of time.

On the big map of the lagoon, every centimetre of the water has a name. We sail along Canale dei Marani around Murano, past the low brick building of the Marco Polo glass factory and a pale pietà that is built into the outside wall of the lighthouse, the mother looks straight ahead and is wearing a crown that is the same doughy colour as the tower. In some places, the mooring posts are tied together in groups of six, sombre sculptures imbued with an enormous power. The lagoon can be a rough place. At Burano, we have to get out and wait, and a little later the next boat for Torcello comes along, I have never understood why, as Torcello is so close, you can already see the tower of the Maria Assunta.

Whenever I am in Venice, I have to go there, it is like passing through a reverse sound barrier, current events are sucked out of you, this is empty and old land, only just above water, you can hardly believe that in 639, when the first church was built, twenty thousand people lived here, the inhabitants of Altinum, who had been driven away from the mainland by Lombard invaders and, after fleeing here, lived on this low land protected by the sea as if in a fortress. Slowly, I make my way along the path beside the narrow canal. On the gentle curve, an accordion player stands beneath a frightfully blue parasol. His place is well chosen, everyone who wants to go to the church has to pass. He is playing Bach, I can still hear the music when I have long since gone by and headed out along a strange path, simply because it is in fact forbidden. PROPRIETÀ PRIVATA, it says twice, and ATTENTI AL CANE, a monster with a wide-open maw that is painted twice, in black and in red. On the door there is a large sign that reads "Designer Food Stylist Wedding Planner" and a German name, but I do not want to get married today and I am afraid of the twice-painted dog, and I certainly have no interest in finding out what a food stylist is. The first scents of autumn are enough for me, the parched blackberry bushes that have wrapped their spiky lianas around the barbed wire. In the distance, I can still see the accordion player's blue parasol like a tropical flower in the landscape, but when there are no people walking along the path the man stops playing and there is only the sound of the wind and the boat, which has departed again.

You come to Torcello for the Byzantine echo of the cathedral. 639, renovated in 864, and then again in 1008, with all kinds of earlier elements still intact. It is one of those rare spaces in which you experience a sense of weight loss, as if, because that whole rarefied space appears to be floating, you too are floating a little across the marble and mosaic of the floors. Here, light has been used as if it is a material, it has lent its colour to the slim columns that raise the building aloft, you are automatically drawn forward, to the iconostasis that rests on even lighter columns above a closed marble balustrade of peacocks and lions facing each other. In the floor, the grave of a bishop, a figure of almost liquid stone lying there asleep in his robes for a thousand years now. If he opens his eyes, he will look out over the altar into a vaulted half-dome of thousands of small golden tiles, the background to a tall, stern, oriental Mary, with diagonally above her in those golden heavens an angel with curiously speckled feet, who is almost touching the simple brick side wall with his wings, which makes you feel that this is the place where the world of Byzantium touches the world of Venice for the first time, a world with which it will later have so much more contact. She, in turn, is looking through the whole church to the opposite wall on the western side, where the Last Judgment is depicted. She can see herself once again there, the stylised, gold-coloured child that she is still carrying in her arms in her golden dome has now become a stern god ruling over the world with a Greek cross in his left hand, and above the head of his mother far beneath him – everything is double in this church – devils and angels are busy weighing souls. It does not end well for the souls that weigh too little, the nameless artists of a thousand years ago have gone to town on this with their little tiles. Some of the damned stand on the right, they have sexless beige bodies with large commas for navels and are doing strange things with their hands, probably out of joy at not having to endure the worse fate of the other doomed folk beside them. Two of these are up to their navels in flames, the third, an older man with dignified grey hair and beard, whom you cannot believe for a moment has ever committed a sin, sits more or less comfortably with his naked body in the high flames of the fire, which is made of long ribbons of red and black tiles. They look strangely unperturbed, as if a fire made out of mosaic cannot hurt, which is likely true. Beneath that, things get worse, and skulls without the rest of their skeletons float through the dark blackness of eternity, with long stringy white worms twisting out of their empty eye sockets. None of this is a deterrent, more of a statement than a threat: if you do not behave, this is what will happen to you. That wall is metres high, with an entire doctrine depicted upon it, theology, redemption, it takes a long time to absorb everything, but when you turn around there is once again that so much more appealing image of the light space of the church itself, Mediterranean light in which guilt, punishment, penance and apocalyptic predictions are immediately resolved, and this continues outside in the autumnal September afternoon of the lagoon. The doctrine depicted on the wall was, at the time when the artists went to work, around a thousand years old, enough to have arrived at such imagery as had never existed before, and, as if I wish to give myself not only a lesson in art history but also in the metamorphoses of religions, as soon as I have returned by vaporetto to the Fondamente Nove, I enter the church of the Gesuiti, where the same faith has clad itself in the Baroque idiom of seven hundred years later, which is perhaps all the more ironic because this Jesuit church has the same name as the one on Torcello, Santa Maria Assunta, but everything that is intimate there, and of antique piety, is extrovert here, theatrical, an externally focused claim to power. Perhaps most beautiful are the dancing figures high on the edge of the façade, as if there is some frivolous discotheque up there, where the saints, robes swishing, are swinging away to an allegro molto by Vivaldi that we down below cannot hear. It is no different inside. On German television they have subtitles for the deaf now, and until someone explained to me that you can remove them with one simple hand movement, I read them with great fascination for a while. When the criminal flees into a church and sits there panting, they say: "panting", and if an organ starts playing in the church, they announce in a conspiratorial tone: "organ music". Now I am the criminal, because as I enter the church soft organ music begins. I cannot help myself, the television viewer in me is now thinking "organ music" and this is accompanied by the feeling that I am walking on subtitles for the deaf. The fact that I am also thinking about Ignatius of Loyola is probably invisible. He founded the Jesuit order as a strict, almost military organisation, but the church that his Italian followers built here is far removed from any strictness. The word had to be central, but the pulpit of vast dimensions that has been built halfway along the left-hand wall, complete with baldachin, crown and drapes of folded stone curtains and tassels, seems remote from any pulpit from which God's word might be proclaimed or explained, and more like a box in a musical theatre. The man – never a woman – who has to speak on that balcony is presented like an opera star, this is so far from the simplicity of Torcello that I can no longer take in the glorious inlaid intarsia and the rest of the Baroque splendour in the enormous grey and white space and I do not walk on to Palma Giovane's paintings in the sacristy either. My head is full, it can no longer make the leap across the centuries and soon after that I am sitting in a wonderful little dark café, where I hear the finest greeting in years. There are only a few people in the place, two older men with sailors' faces, a couple of young lovers, the man behind the bar, who is talking to a friend and who has just brought me a large glass of almost purple wine with a bowl of black olives. I am clearly the only foreigner and I am sitting there, pondering all the guises that the Church as an institution has assumed over the centuries, and where it will go from here, when a cheery man comes in and, with a radiant smile, calls out to no-one in particular: *Buona sera a quasi tutti!* Including me, there are seven people sitting among the big wine barrels in the small, dark room. *Quasi tutti* means nearly everyone. So whom does he not wish to greet? I do not have a complex about this, but have I immediately been identified as a tourist? In the centre of Amsterdam, I sometimes have a loathing for all the tourists who get under your feet, and in Venice it must be a hundred times worse. Good evening to almost everyone! I should try it one day in my own local in the Jordaan.

An old paperback. Paper that has turned brownish, which I always think of as war paper. At the front of the book, a greyish map of the lagoon. In three places, numbers have been written by hand on the map. I have not seen the book for years, but the numbers are clearly in my handwriting. It is called *Dead Lagoon*, was published in 1994, and I remember nothing else about it now, but I do know that the protagonist is a police commissario whose name is Aurelio Zen. Now, Zen is already a wonderful name for someone who has visited a Zen monastery, but in Venice that name has an additional significance. Let's start with page 141. That number is by the town of Chioggia. A little higher up on the map I have written the number 221 beside a narrow strip of grey drawn in the lagoon, with the Adriatic Sea on the right of the map, and to the left the part of the lagoon that is called Laguna Morta, with the Fondi dei Sette Morti. So the Dead Lagoon and the Depths of the Seven Dead – not very cosy. "I Murazzi" and "Pellestrina" are written there, which, the book says on page 221, is "a bizarre community three kilometres long and a stone's throw wide, built on a sandbank in the shadow of the *murazzi*, the massive sea defences erected by the Republic three hundred years earlier".

But perhaps I should explain something first. Two of the best-known thriller writers who focus on Venice are Michael Dibdin and Donna Leon. I enjoy reading thrillers, but I am most fond of the ones about Venice, as I feel that by reading them I understand more about the city. After all, they take you to all kinds of places. Shipyards, hospitals, palazzi – you find crime and corruption everywhere. And when I read something like that, something about strange and ancient sea defences, I want to go there. It is one of the ways in which I penetrate the secrets of a city.

The name of Leon's commissario is Brunetti, and, since films have been made of her books, he even has a face. Such things can be terrible if the character in the film does not correspond to your own imagining, but in this case it worked. Brunetti, his beautiful wife Paola, who teaches English literature at the University of Venice and is of noble Venetian descent, their two teenage children, but most of all the mistress of the Internet, the exquisite, flower-buying Signorina Elettra, the extremely intelligent secretary of the oh-so-stupid Vice-Questore Patta, have almost become a kind of family to me, even though they do not exist.

The situation with Aurelio Zen is a little different, but it started with him: as everything that cannot be done on a boat in Venice must happen on foot, it is easy to follow the steps of Brunetti and Zen, which explains those numbers that I write in the books, so that later, map in hand, I can see where they walked. As neither commissario exists, they have never met, but their workplace does exist. And this time I am planning to visit it. Back to Zen. He is in Chioggia, about two hours by boat from the Schiavoni, and he is not alone. On page 140 someone has said to him "Unlike you, we're true Venetians, and proud of it!", to which Zen has murmured back in dialect, "But I hear your granny screws Albanians" and now we are on page 141 and Zen is beginning an interrogation.

> The policewoman straightened up. "Ready," she told Zen, who nodded. The reels of the recorder started to revolve. Zen recited the date, the time, the place.
>
> "Present are Vice-Questore Aurelio Zen en Sottotenente . . ."
>
> He glanced inquiringly at the policewoman, a svelte but rather severe brunette who contrived to make her

duty-issue uniform look as though it sported a designer label from one of the better houses.

"Nunziata, Pia," she replied, having paused the tape.

"... and Sottotenente Pia Nunziata," Zen continued.

Perhaps I would like to follow those two now, but it is not my book, and I do not think Michael Dibdin would approve. In my own story, I go in search of the police headquarters where both Zen and Brunetti work. In fiction, non-existent police officers sometimes have real offices and, if I am not mistaken, that real office is by Campo San Lorenzo, opposite the abandoned church of San Lorenzo and next to a home for the elderly. Everything is as it should be. The vaporetto has taken me from my monastery on the small island of San Giorgio to the San Zaccaria stop and, protected by those two saints, I go in search of the third saint and, of course, I promptly get lost again. Venetians have deliberately created dead-end streets. The shadowy alleyway close to the Zaccaria, which has no name on the map, cannot be right, I have to return to the square in front of the Zaccaria (a walker in Venice is someone who boldly retraces his footsteps) and then valiantly I wander on, with the church behind me, across Campo San Provolo to Fondamente dell'Osmarin, thinking to myself that there must be a story attached to all those names and wanting to know what each one is, turn left before the bridge that goes to Calle

Madonna and separates the water into Rio dei Greci and Rio San Lorenzo, and then I am there, and everything is fine. Follow me in my chaos, and you will see it is all correct. Here, in this whitewashed office, Aurelio Zen worked, and I think Brunetti still works here. Those who do not believe in books have no business being here. Polizia di Stato, Questura, Commissariato di San Marco it says on the wall. Under one of the two video cameras, the white plaster has flaked off, as if the building is in its underwear. I see a sign in the entrance hall: *Sub Lege Libertas*. Freedom under the Law. All I have to do is enter the building and I will turn into paper, something to which a writer cannot object. I would like to drink an espresso with Zen, and a grappa with Brunetti, I would like to see which flowers the beautiful Elettra has chosen at the Rialto for the vice-questore today, peer up at the windows at which Brunetti so often stands looking out over the campo or pondering the mysterious web of corruption, small and large, in which this city is caught, and which is so mercilessly well described by Donna Leon that her books are published in all kinds of languages, but not in Italian. I do not know if this is out of fear with a capital F or whether she simply wishes to continue living in peace in her favourite city. With Brunetti's eyes on my back, I cross the bridge to the empty square, but when I want to enter the church I find myself stepping into a curious ruin, a work of art in itself, an apotheosis of decay, as if a great but negative

artist has been at work here and has made a pact with Time itself. In the First World War, San Lorenzo was hit by a bomb, and it never recovered. I peer into mysterious depths, walls laid bare, underground wooden partitions, an empty tabernacle, an excavated tiled floor. Between the columns on the left and right, once the colour of porphyry, two other columns, tortured and covered with dust, the walls look like Arte Povera, it is incredible what nuances of brown and grey can be introduced by slow decay. The garlands and the angels' heads, the rusty scaffolding, sometimes disintegration says more about a style and a building than perfection. Marco Polo was buried here once upon a time, but his grave has never been found, he is still on his voyages.

Antique Tourism

Wobble. Wibblewobble. Wibblewobblewibblewobble.

I have finally plucked up the courage. Ten times in Venice and in a gondola for the first time. As I drink my coffee early in the morning on the corner of the Procuratie Nuove, they stand beside me: the gondolieri. Big conversations about yesterday's match in their impenetrable Venetian dialect. It is cold on the water, a hot *cappuccio* helps. Outside, their slim, black, bird boats are lined up, the birds' heads (they are birds' heads – take a good look) pointing at the island where I am staying. Why did I never want to do it? Because it is the ultimate Venetian cliché?

That would be childish. Because of the faces of the people in the gondolas? What is it about those faces? The unbearable bliss of what has been achieved, the absolute Venetian baptism, which means you will always belong here? In the gondola, along with Thomas Mann, Mary McCarthy, Franz Kafka, Henry James, Ezra Pound. Louis Couperus? *Ich bin auch ein Berliner*, something like that? Or, if our neighbours in Kansas, Bielefeld, Wakayama, Novosibirsk, Barneveld could see us now – is it that expression? As if, down there on the water, they have draped the entire city around themselves like a cloak, a still yet swaying moment of fulfilment, swelling watery whispers around you in the quieter canals, the unseen man behind you, the ferryman with his strong, rhythmic movements. And yet, most people have not found the right facial expression, even though they are doing their best. This can only be because they know they are going nowhere and will soon arrive back at their point of departure. What kind of expression should you wear when the people in the vaporetto, who are actually going somewhere, are looking at you?

I had never done anything more than the traghetto, which is also a gondola, but just from one side to the other of the Canal Grande. A shaky climb aboard, the steady hand of the ferryman taking hold of your arm, trying to stand so you do not lose your balance or perching instead on the narrow plank so as not to lose face. Face or balance – that is what it is about. No, I had never done it before. Last year, when it snowed in Venice and we had a small apartment by Campo San Samuele, down an alleyway in the back part of what must once have been a grand palazzo (a dark, hidden space behind bars, with a dog that always barked when we came in, and barely a view of the water), I had seen Japanese people passing by early in the morning, huddled beneath umbrellas, snow on their hats and scarves, beaming with joy. The gondoliere sang about the sun as he wiped the snow out of his eyes. *O sole mio*. I admired him. The boat came past slowly and I knew they would never forget that journey, I wished that I knew the Japanese word for "never". If you have not been in a gondola, you have never been to Venice. Everyone takes a photograph of everyone else: proof. You buy the holiday in Japan including your gondola ride. But was that any reason for me not to do it? Soaked Chinese people in the rain, Americans with a bottle of Prosecco? I had tried to find a rational excuse for my nonsense, a gondola is a means of transportation, which you take when you are going somewhere, as in the old days, when there were no vaporetti. Just bobbing around a bit, that could never have been the intention, even though I always wander aimlessly about the city on foot. An even blacker gondola than usual, with a coffin under a gold-embroidered cloth, on its way to San Michele, the island of the dead, that was real, the essence of transportation. All the rest was tourism, affectation, theatre, something for other people.

And now? Now we ourselves were the other people, sitting in a gondola, that shaky climb aboard, too heavy, the little boat tilting, but the practised hand assists clumsy bodies, deposits them on cushions, the journey can begin and at once the world is changed, taking place above you,

you see not faces but shoes on the quays beside you, the buildings stretch out and suddenly you discover all kinds of things you have never paid attention to before; a gentle swell holds sway over the city, you see the walls as living skin, injuries, wounds, scars, healing, old age, history, black seaweed, green seaweed, the mysterious underside of bridges, marble and masonry, the other boats, life afloat in a city of stone and water. In a low voice the gondoliere recites the names of churches and large buildings, as if an elderly priest were praying a litany to which you do not have to listen. I try to follow where we are on the map but soon lose track. Sometimes, when we go around a sharp corner, he lets out a loud "Oi!", as if we are in mortal danger, but I have long since surrendered and, like a child in the womb, I listen to the murmuring of the amniotic water and wish never to be born again.

A memory. A winter's day. It has snowed on Piazza San Marco, but the snow soon melted. I am standing in one of the galleries, looking out at the wet square, thinking I can see the meltwater slowly running away but, as in Nijhoff's poem, the reality turns out to be different: I do not see what I see, because, as if there is a spring in the middle of the stones of the square, I watch the water rising in a few places, as if the city is porous. I have not heard the sirens that warn of seriously high water, so it cannot be bad, and yet I cannot take my eyes off it. There should be earth beneath it, not water, a city is not a ship. Or is it? I am standing on stone, I am not Jesus. But am I really standing on stone? In the distance, I can see people lugging those peculiar boardwalks – elongated wooden structures on metal legs, which allow you to continue your route just above the surface of the water without having to wade through it. It can rise to half a metre, and if that happens, narrow paths are built with those boardwalks, upon which pedestrians struggle to pass one another. The mud that comes from the bottom of the lagoon is black, water of the dead from the Lethe, the river of oblivion. I have stood there when they were dredging somewhere, with one of those claws that digs into the depths and vomits forth pitch-black mud, along with all manner of objects from the realm of the dead that have assumed the same colour as water in mourning, in a counter-city that lies down below, biding its time.

When the water has receded, the platforms remain as a reminder that this can all change, that the full moon of the Romantic paintings sometimes, in an ill humour, takes charge of the water. And because, since the last ice age, there has been ten times more water than land in the lagoon, people in this battle zone between rivers and sea have had to survive as best they can. The thought of the Netherlands and the sea is, of course, not far distant. The branches of the Po Delta brought sand from the mountains of the hinterland, the currents of the sea fought against it, sandbanks formed that wanted to enclose the lagoon, the delta's tributaries had to be diverted to prevent the whole area from silting up and to pour fresh water into the sea through three openings. In an aerial photograph taken from a great height, the lagoon resembles a living organism, the waterways as the blood vessels, the rerouted rivers to the north and south as arteries, the industrial estates of Mestre and Porto Marghera as large tumours, and Venice itself a jewel casually discarded and lost. This lends the surrounding marshes the air of a royal robe for a king on a shaky throne of Istrian sandstone, the heroic variety of stone that can withstand the voracity of seawater, just like the pines that also came from Istria and, as in Amsterdam, are rammed deep into sand and clay to carry the weight of houses and palaces. Whoever achieved all of that could go forth and conquer the world.

Stories in Pictures I

Tiepolo in the Doge's Palace

THREE FIGURES AGAINST THE BLUE OF THE SKY. THE trident tells you which god is meant. But he is not holding it, the curious weapon that is his emblem, it is lying half across his back and that of the dark-haired young woman in a deep-green dress whose head is so close to his. The person who is in fact holding his weapon cannot be seen. It is the most human portrait I know of him. He is large and strong, half-naked, the long hair black, the beard wild and grey, his right eye is in love, the other cannot be seen but that one is enough, his young skin is brown and gleaming, a few chest hairs, his working hands darker in colour, as with farmers and fishermen. He is holding them around the horn of plenty that he is now emptying out before the blonde woman in the crown. Coins, a bright-red piece of coral, strings of pearls, it is all painted so fantastically that you think you can see the images on the coins, figures in the gleam of gold and silver, a treasure, pouring out past his mighty knee and onto her gold brocade dress. There is no doubt about it, he is not making an

GONDOLE

obligatory tribute: he is giving out of love and Venice is the woman to whom he is giving all of this. With a long pale hand that emerges from beneath the ermine, she points and looks at him with an expression that lies between astonishment and something like fear. The sexual connotation is undeniable, she is beautiful, the left hand with which she is loosely holding her sceptre rests on the head of a gigantic dog with a monstrous maw, she reclines in all her finery, taking up two-thirds of the painting, so that it seems as if he is racing towards her like a big wave, heaven knows what might happen next between the sea god and his favourite city. Seen in the Doge's Palace, in the Room of the Four Doors, where the ambassadors had to wait for an audience.

Carpaccio in the Museo Correr

It says something about Ruskin that he called Carpaccio's two women the Courtesans. Women of easy virtue (from the better classes), as my dictionary tells me, in case I had any doubt. Why did Ruskin think they were a more elevated sort of prostitute? The clothing of the two women is Venetian, luxurious, their hairstyles sophisticated, their jewellery not excessive, but present. One of the women has a voluptuous décolletage, but that was not uncommon. Whatever possessed Ruskin? His Victorian prudishness? Legend has it that he had spent so much time looking at polished marble nudes that he had the fright of his life on his wedding night when he saw his wife's pubic hair. And yet I believe it was because of other elements that can be observed in this fabulous painting. Both women are looking straight ahead, turned away from the viewer, both are looking with an empty gaze, apparently at nothing. And even though there is plenty going on, it seems as if nothing is moving, it is as if they are waiting, an often-lengthy occupation with which courtesans are not unfamiliar.

So what are we actually seeing? Two doves, two dogs, maybe the legs of one of those dogs or of a third that cannot be seen. The woman with the cleavage is holding a long thin stick in her right hand, which the larger dog is gripping between its sharp teeth. The laws of perspective do not reveal to me whether the two front legs that I can see in the bottom left of the painting, one of which rests on an unfolded note that I cannot read, belong to the same dog: however, the shade of the fur leads me to suspect that this is the case. In her left hand, the woman is holding the thin right front leg of a little mutt, which is sitting upright and looking at me impudently. The other woman appears to have her feet in two enormous green embroidered slippers, but it could just be the billowing bottom of her dress. These are things that art history knows, and maybe it also knows the meaning of the crow-like bird sitting on the ground directly in front of her, lifting up its three-toed foot. This woman, too, has that empty, staring gaze at nothing, which for convenience I will call modern. In her right hand she has a linen or silk cloth, her elbow is resting on the high marble balustrade beside a pomegranate, the symbol of love and fertility (that much I do remember). It is unclear whether the boy, whose head does not yet reach above the balustrade, is also aware of that fact. In any case, his whole attention is on the peacock, which clearly he would like to pet. Next to the peacock are two of those women's shoes that were fashionable at the time and which look as if they were impossible to walk in.

This painting hangs in the Museo Correr and if you get the chance to stand quietly in front of it for a while, it becomes only more silent around those women. According to more recent theories, they are waiting for their men to return from the hunt, but that does not solve the riddle of the silence. Clothing and objects situate the painting in time, but the emptiness of the gaze and the little dog's haughty dismissal smell more like my own era. That dog knows too much, and we know each other.

Guardi

The city I left a few weeks ago has turned into paper. Now that I have left, the big Guardi exhibition has finally come to the Museo Correr. Francesco Guardi, who during his lifetime always had to let Canaletto go first, even though he knew that he, of course, was better because he could bring the city to life, because he released the palazzi from the stasis in which the other painter had captured them for all eternity, because he made the water breathe, made the cries of all those men on their ships audible, and because his clouds were people who moved over water and city in such a way that you want to give them names. A friend who knows my obsessions has sent me a copy of *El País* and a page from the *New York Times*, both of which are about the exhibition. So I am still a little in Venice after all.

The black and white of the grainy newspaper pages makes me see the paintings as they should not be seen, stricken by an incurable greyness, but still I fill in the colours with memory and nostalgia. Thin and a little transparent, the painter stands in the only known portrait of him, brush in hand as if he has something to prove, the colours on his palette, white and dark lines, feminine hands, bright eyes that would retain everything they saw. The city, the city and once again the city, a liquid city of water and boats, a stone city of palaces, and also everything that happened behind all those blank walls, the city in the city, the vanity fair of the Ridotto, an eddy of sophistication and lust around the gaming tables, a soft scent of decay heralding the gradual end. His paintings have returned home, heaven knows they were homesick for the city where Guardi, forever in Canaletto's shadow, once tried to sell them on Piazza San Marco. From all over the world they have flown to the Correr, forty museums and institutions have released them for a few months, I cannot wait to see them. In the grey of the newspaper in front of me, I look at the waterfront of Giudecca, where I so recently walked, I see the small island where I stayed, clasped between light and shadow, a distant twilight where I could be one of the shadows that populate Guardi's paintings. This city has scarcely changed since his day, so it seems as if in these paintings the time that has passed has been cancelled out. I am no longer where I am and yet I am there, I have turned into paint and I am walking there in the now of 1760, where he has painted me, a man in strange clothes sitting on the steps in front of the church I will walk past two centuries later, a twentieth-century Dutchman in the most serene of all republics.

Went away and came back again. It is the same season, but everything is a bit darker, greyer, colder. Now I am not staying on the small island, but in the city, and the perspective changes. The sounds are different, footsteps at night, voices in the morning, mingling with sleep and half-sleep, drawing you into the world.

The hotel is small, the room is small, intimate. To read at night I have to put the small old-fashioned lamp at an angle, so that the book catches a little light. I read about the doges, whose graves I will visit in the Frari and in Giovanni e Paolo. In those churches they hang high on the walls in their sarcophagi, as if they wanted to withdraw from the world of men and were in a hurry to get to heaven. I have visited them in previous years and wondered if I would like that too, sleeping for all eternity halfway up a church wall with that strange echo of a Phrygian cap on my head, my stone hands folded, power and intrigue renounced, surrounded by images of virtues or the paraphernalia of war, still powerful in a helpless way, but only as a dead man, a paradox in stone. My hotel is opposite Santa Maria del Giglio, which is also known as Zobenigo here, my room is directly across from its façade, but it was evening when I arrived, and ungratefully I noted the concierge's remark about a beautiful view, since there is no water nearby. A view in Venice means water, I must have thought, and my mistake becomes clear when I open first the curtains and then the shutters, as my view from the third floor is the façade of the Giglio itself, men in wigs, angels of unbridled dimensions, allegorical figures, generals, sea battles, maps of cities, human or divine creatures of various sizes, pediments, cornices, spandrels, friezes, pilasters, frames, corbels, putti, an unceasing scene that will keep me occupied for three mornings. I have never had a relationship with a façade from my bed before, but now it is unavoidable. As soon as I open my eyes and the shutters, I see the small square below, the newspaper kiosk, the passers-by on their way to the vaporetto. The façade does not appreciate my eyes taking that little excursion, it demands not only my undivided attention, but also a specific kind of focus, never again will I be so close to it, at eye level, but where should I begin? The first day it was the twins. Have you ever looked out from your bed at stone twins? They are somewhere on the left-hand side, close to my window, and they are so similar that they must be twins, half-naked men, the one on the left holding in his left hand a large loincloth, which apparently continues behind his back, as there is also part of that cloth in his right hand. They look serious, are about forty-five years old, have sturdy Renaissance bodies on their way to Baroque, on their heads they are wearing Doric capitals, as if it is nothing. I think they are sandstone but they could be gypsum that is pretending to be marble. The man on the right is also holding a cloth which is designed to serve as a backdrop for a coat of arms with a two-headed eagle, but the more I look, the more everything begins to seem like an extremely sophisticated examination for an architecture student who is supposed to know the names of all those details, for whom words such as salients, entablature, pediment, architrave, archivolt have no secrets. Everything in this world has a name, from carnivorous plants and the very least of spiders up to and including extinct skeletons from prehistoric times and the cartouches on the façade opposite, we need to know what we are talking about after all, even though that does not diminish the mysteries.

It is clear to me that I need to get out of bed, if only to reduce the insane perspective that I have from my window to a more human scale, although I do not know if it will work. I can just about handle the proud man in the middle of the façade with his knickerbockers and something like a military baton and a very strange upwardly expanding bowl on the overly exuberant curls of his wig, but how is he ever to couple with one of the gigantic female figures up at the top, assuming that he wants to? Their sizes do not match, he would drown with all his pride in their plaster embrace. And what about my own size? It is only when I am standing on the street with the façade above me that I can attempt to gauge it. Four men of stone stand there more or less opposite me, but still high enough to look down on me. Wigs, lightly fluttering clothes in the wind that is not there today, above their heads the paraphernalia of learning, power, wealth, position. No doubt about it, they are worthy of regard, and for the first time I hear the word in its true meaning as I think it. They deserve to be regarded, to be looked at and respected, they knew it and their contemporaries knew it too, and if you want humankind in the future to know it, then you build a church. The brothers Barbaro – Giovanni Maria, Marino, Francesco and Carlo. The lonely brother in the middle of the façade is Antonio, 1627–78, procurator of Crete, Captain of the Gulf and *provveditore* of Candia. If you are a Barbaro, you still rule three centuries later, you have the sea battles you won against the Turks and the two-dimensional maps of the cities you governed in relief all around you, and your brothers with their titles at street level by your feet. One of those statues of brothers or sons is even reading now, no time wasted here.

The hotel concierge gives me a small book about the church, but it is not for sale and I can consult it only briefly. The façade is a design by Giuseppe Sardo, the maps are of Rome, Padua, Corfu, Candia, which is now called Heraklion, the war at sea is depicted with rigged flagships and galleons, wild waves and rowers with long oars, turning the whole façade into a slow-motion movie. When I look up the Barbaros online, I find them in every century, all the way back to Nicolasa, who in 1470 married Bayezid II, the sultan of the Ottoman Empire. In Venice, the East was never far away.

I read in the *Gazzettino* that at around 11 o'clock tomorrow the water may rise to 1.30 m, tension is high, everyone is talking about it. The boardwalks are out in preparation, but I know that at around that time I should be wading along Calle del Traghetto with my suitcases. At about six, the siren goes, a sound that always reminds me of the war, you never shake it off, and certainly not this siren, it proclaims calamity and danger, screaming that the Huns are advancing tonight.

You remember that this city lies in the water, connected to the rest of the world only by a narrow bridge, as if you are on a ship that might sink. I open the shutters, it is pitch dark, the sound now wails into the room, whines a little before falling silent, the kind of silence in which you hear all kinds of things that are not there. Then a second sound begins, a strange melody repeated over and over, a mysterious mechanical singing that echoes off the façade of the Giglio opposite me, as if it wishes to contradict or deny the impending disaster with this harmonious humming, but it does not work. The sense of threat increases because of the mystery of that sound, the constant obsessive repetition, until that too dies away and the silence without voices and footsteps once again takes possession of the city. When I wake up again, a couple of hours later, and open the window, I see that Antonio Barbaro has not changed position, and Glory and the cardinal Virtues are still sitting unmoved on the arch that forms the top of the façade, Fame, Virtue and Wisdom have not moved from their places, all is right with the world. The newspaper kiosk is open, I see no water anywhere, the moon, the tides and the water have reminded the city of its vulnerability, tomorrow the *Gazzettino* will write that it was all a false alarm, until the next time.

A lesson I learned in Berlin when the Wall was still there. If you cannot go out, then you look inward for distance, in unfamiliar districts, strange parks, nondescript squares, courtyards with large rubbish bins, dilapidated façades. Likewise, in Venice, I seek out the empty parts of the city, the narrow streets near San Giobbe, the alleys around the Salizzada Stretta or San Giuseppe di Castello, or, as is the case now, on the other tip of Giudecca. I have no reason to be there, nothing to look for, and that is precisely what I am looking for: nothing. I have extricated myself from the excesses of the city and feel as if I can wander aimlessly in an unburdened no-man's-land, having walked along the Fondamenta Sant'Eufemia and the Fondamenta San Biagio, I allowed myself to get lost, retraced my footsteps, kept coming back to the water, seeing no-one, a light drizzle, no trees and yet a gentle rustling. Where is that sound coming from? I stand very still, hear a boat passing in the distance and wait until it is quiet again so that I can hear that sound once more. I was scarcely paying attention to where I was walking, and now I have come to a narrow waterway that could be Rio Morto and still I can hear that sound, a swishing, the movement of very many quiet things, almost a whispering, but not of people, the noise of paper, a newspaper in the wind, but there is no wind. On the narrow quay that is not a real quay there is a boat covered with a black tarpaulin. Now I am sure, the sound is coming from there, if

I stand very still I can hear it clearly, a hoarse rustling, a soft hissing, but what is it? When I see that no-one is watching, I dare to lift the tarpaulin a little and unveil the mystery, hundreds and hundreds of little black crabs crawling over one another, their legs scrabbling over the fragile armour of the others, a black, slightly shiny mass teeming and sliding over each other, the catch of a fisherman from the black water of the lagoon, mud-coloured, looking for a way out with their claws interlocking under and over one another, a Venetian melody for a thousand crabs, a song from the Styx.

The book on my table is a hundred years old. Large, the pages slightly discoloured and sprinkled with what antiquarian booksellers refer to as foxing, a little like the liver spots on my hands, which in the Dutch region of Twente are known as "graveyard flowers". It is a book by my hero, Louis Couperus, along with Multatuli one of the surviving greats who date back to the nineteenth century, a wonderful novelist and also someone who wrote brilliantly about his travels. The cover has a design with Jugendstil elements, flowers and strange creatures floating around the central section with the title: *Uit blanke steden onder blauwe lucht* (From White Cities under Blue Skies). The style is mannerist, a little antiquarian, evocative, still readable, a style that fits with my own origins, by which I mean that I read Couperus from a young age, his books about Indonesia and about Japan took me into the distance I was looking for, he travelled slowly and that is also how he wrote, his full stops at the end of a sentence were the place he had reserved for the reader's imagination. The first chapter in his book is about Venice, and what I just wrote is literally confirmed there: "Because this city is a dream and a fable; she is not real, she does not exist . . . We imagine her! She is a *fata morgana*, she is born in pearly splendour, she rises in the splendour of gold, she swoons in violet night shadows."

No, you cannot write like that any longer, touched by symbolism and impressionism, slow and a little sultry, with all manner of little touches to convey every possible nuance of the light, or of the water, or of a work of art, but I can still read like that, because by reading Couperus I am still in the same city, and yet a century earlier, a city in which a scent of the recently vanished *fin de siècle* still lingers, a slower and more leisurely Venice. It is not clear whether a reader in another language will be able to read what I read in the same way, new translations cannot do justice to the antique and mannered nature of this language. Over the past century, Proust has been translated into English three times, while the French still have to make do with language that is a hundred years old – I have no problem with that, but the generation of smartphones and iPads requires a different pace, fewer words, less ornamentation, and that makes the city a different one, as a change in language also implies a change in seeing. I enjoy walking around here a century ago. Of course, the absence of cars helps, while on the other hand a certain haste among the people proves a hindrance. Couperus had no such problems, he sails in his gondola along the "velvet gloom of small canals over ink-dark waters" and then returns to his ink comparison and says "across that ink, rippled red here and there with the sudden gleam of a lantern, through that haze of velvet, through that chill breath of damp and autumn, our gondola glided into the mystery of the sombre night and it was as if, in narrow distances, between black palaces, out of the waters shimmering with blood, ghosts rose up, their long, dripping-wet veils dragging across the inky surface, and dissolved into mist and cloud . . ." Fine, admittedly impressionism, here and there a dash of black, a dot of red applied to the swaying water, the lighting was different in those days too, and if no water taxis sailed past you, perhaps you would be more likely to see a ghost in the half-light half-darkness of the yellowish lamps than we are now, but essentially if you allow yourself the time to read, you *see* every image he evokes, particularly when he, with a modern cinematic twist, takes a leap.

> Suddenly . . .
>
> Suddenly, after cry upon cry from the paddling gondoliers, the lagoon opened up before us, the gondola turned and . . .
>
> A magical sight spread out in a swarm of lights before our eyes . . .

Nothing that he describes after that has changed, not the Piazzetta, not the bronze lion of San Marco, and not the light on the lagoon either, or the sudden view of that "strange, wondrous building, an enchanted castle, a peculiar magical architecture [. . .] the Doge's Palace . . . [. . .] the dwelling place of a Caliph . . ."

When I look up from my book, the century between him and me has evaporated, that is what I saw for myself just a few days ago, and when I close my eyes I see him sitting in his Venetian hotel and hear his pen scribbling the words I have just read.

Two Poems

I

HE STILL REMEMBERED LATER THAT THE CANAL STANK in 1934, recalling the smell of the brackish water together with the fug of fried scampi. From the window of his hotel he had been able to see the typists in the office across the way, he pictured that now too. It had been a strange afternoon. The woman who had a room in the same hotel had come a long way, and this had been their view, a Venetian landscape. They must, he thought later, when he wrote it down, not have seen the same even though both of them saw the same. A woman who prefers to listen to Gesualdo and Bach looks in a different way than a man who loves not only opera but also the most banal repertoire. God yes, and the clock had said five even though it was only four, so they had run, first across Piazza San Marco, where Florian's was empty, then along Riva degli Schiavoni, past Trattoria Paganelli, which had been recommended to them by a penny-pinching Florentine painter. They had two rooms in their hotel, not even next to each other, he could remember that too, of course, and the way she had dashed past the following morning without even looking at his Ranzoni painting. And then thinking back to the wonderful conversation in Florence as they were walking down the steps of the Oltrarno to the large square. But in the now of his memory they were still passing through the Venice of then, a summer from before the war, unbearable heat, pigeons, photographers, the sheer weight of the Biennale catalogue they had not looked inside, not even once. They had returned on the vaporetto, then wandered back along the quay, birdseed beneath their feet. They had bought souvenirs, sunglasses and postcards. Yes, it had been 1934 when their earlier selves had walked there, too young or too unfamiliar for a city that depends on tourists and old lovers.

2

I do not know where it was exactly, but certainly by the water. It is still morning, maybe a little sun through a light mist, and behind the houses the greater light of the lagoon. The passer-by sees an older man, perhaps the same man who is remembering a woman in the previous story, and the summer of 1934, in conversation with a concierge. At least, that is what he looks like, and it is not so much the old man who is speaking, but the concierge, who is holding the door half open, half shut with one hand, and making gestures of refusal with the other. A Venetian scene, the loud voice of the concierge, who is using a great many words in order not to allow the other man to enter. In different costumes, perhaps an excerpt from a play by Goldoni. Someone is not there, does not wish to be disturbed; the other man insists, argues. The older man could be a bailiff, or an unwelcome family member, the passer-by has already walked on, but not without overhearing this and that. Maybe he made up a story about what was actually taking place there. If he was a foreigner, perhaps he had heard the word Hemingway, or Pound, who was very well known in Venice. But if the passer-by had been an Italian, perhaps he would have recognised the older man, the opera critic from the *Corriere della Sera*, who also writes poetry. Eugenio Montale. Perhaps that is how it happened, but how would I know? Am I acquainted with these people? No, not the concierge, but I know Montale from his poems, and I have his poems with me, here, in Venice. A Penguin edition from 2002, with translations into English of the most important poems, by various different translators. There is a photograph of the poet on the cover. His right hand raised in the photographer's light, a lit cigarette between index and middle fingers, an immaculate white shirt, maybe handmade, a deep-black tie, a dressing gown with a delicate pattern, maybe silk. Distinguished. The heavy face in meditation, as if he has just heard or thought of something that he wants to ponder for a long time. This is a head that has lived long, heard a lot, seen a lot. Thought a lot. A poetry mill. The head of the man who wrote *Satura*, poems with a different tone from the mythical and sometimes enigmatic poems of before, of *Ossi di Seppia*, or *Le Occasioni*, in which Dante and Cavalcanti sometimes resounded as distant echoes from a venerated past. These new poems are more worldly, anecdotal, direct. They talk about a life after a previous life, sometimes they are also memories of that previous life, not cynical, but with a clairvoyant distance. In one of those poems, Montale describes his visit to Hemingway in Venice, a poem almost like reportage, all the details photographically recorded, the scene that my passer-by could have seen, that the reader that I am can see. I also know in which year the event occurred, it is written in the front of the same Penguin edition, it was 1954. In January that year, there was a false report that Hemingway had died in a plane crash and, in March, Montale, who was not yet a Nobel laureate, came to Venice to interview Hemingway for the *Corriere della Sera*. Hemingway had won the Pulitzer for *The Old Man and the Sea* the previous year, and in 1954 he would win the Nobel Prize.

The older man from my Venetian story attempts to impress the concierge. He exaggerates a little, a journalist with an assignment, who wants to get inside; the concierge with the features of one of Dante's devils resists, he is under strict instructions, the American writer must not be disturbed. But the other man insists, mentions Pound, who is supposedly his friend, and is clearly himself someone who deserves special treatment. He is dressed plainly but elegantly, he knows the right people. And this is Italy. The concierge rings upstairs. They are still standing in the doorway. Patches of light in the gently moving water. A vaporetto passing by. There is no sound more Venetian. Through it, the voice of the concierge, the silences when the other voice, the one up above, speaks. Then – success. The visitor may go upstairs. Much later, the poem will relate exactly what the poet saw upstairs, that day in March. The writer is still in bed, under a fur cover. All the visitor can see is his eyes and the eczema on the surrounding skin. Two or three empty Merlot bottles, from that morning or the night before, harbingers of what will follow, later, downstairs in the restaurant.

There the conversation is not about the writer, but about people they both know, the bookshop Shakespeare and Company, Adrienne Monnier, Sylvia Beach, rue de l'Odéon, Larbaud, the wild 1920s, the tumultuous 1950s, their own time.

Paris a pigsty, London ditto, New York *stinks*, they have the plague there. And there is nothing to hunt in the marshes here. No wild ducks and no girls, not even a single idea for a book *like that book*, the book that won the prize. No more strokes of luck, no old man and no real sea. They make a list of friends they have in common, but the visitor does not really want to listen. Everything is rotten, says the writer, everything. Almost in tears, he asks the visitor not to send any more visitors, certainly not visitors who are like him – it is even worse when they are intelligent. Then he gets up, wraps himself in his dressing gown again, embraces the poet and says *adieu.*

He lived for another two years, and upon his second death he had no time left to read his obituaries. The poem that describes the visit was published in 1962 in *Satura.* It is called "Venetian Piece". Thirteen years later, the visitor himself would win the Nobel Prize. The passer-by in Venice who imagined all this after reading one man's poem about the other believes that he really saw it all happen.

The Lost Last Supper

WHEN YOU HEAR THE WORD INQUISITION, YOU THINK of Spain, heretics in strange tall pointed hats, the stake, forced confessions, horrifying images that make the words Holy Inquisition a cruel oxymoron. It is less well known that there were also inquisitors in Venice who could make life rather difficult for people. In the Accademia, there is an enormous painting by Paolo Veronese that was once the subject of an interrogation of the painter by three Venetian inquisitors. And because the Inquisition, like the Gestapo and the Stasi, put everything in writing, we know what was asked and answered that day, July 18, 1573. Veronese was then forty-five years old and at the height of his fame. What was the case against him? The painter had been commissioned by the Dominicans to make a particularly large painting for the refectory of their monastery, which was to depict the Last Supper. He must have enjoyed himself, as it is a gigantic canvas with his familiar majestic and colourful figures at a table upon and around which all kinds of things are happening.

One of the privileges of painters is that they can dream up a sky. We do not know what kind of weather it was on the day he devised that sky, but the heaven we see through the three large openings of the magnificent building in which he had the banquet take place was a glorious, vibrant expanse of radiant blue, with greyish, gold-rimmed clouds moving across, lending its own relief to the architectural linearity of the classical buildings in the background, which were modern at the time. I have tried to count the people who were present at the feast, dwarves, halberdiers, servants, the high and mighty, hangers-on, men in turbans, black men, but it is impossible. There were at least fifty of them, not including the sculpted angels perched on the round arches of those openings, and the people through the windows and on the landings and the balconies of the adjacent buildings. The table is standing in an open room, framed by two lines of six Corinthian columns, everything indicates luxury and wealth. Canary yellow, scarlet, that is how the guests – apparently all men – have dressed themselves, vivid colours that fit well with their rhetorical postures. Surrounded by what must have been a huge noise, Jesus sits with his faithful disciples almost off to one side, as if he is not actually a part of it, and yet his charisma makes him the secret and intimate centre of what seems to be a big and chaotic party. It is peaceful where he is sitting. He is young, is talking to a young man beside him, there is no way of knowing what he is saying at that moment, this is not revealed until later. Peter cuts the meat and passes it to the other side of the table, there is a man with a bloody nose, and a dog is also in attendance, Judas of course, the wealthy host, who was called Simon, a few halberdiers, German guests (in those days they were considered as Protestants and therefore heretics) and, naturally, the domestic staff.

Hardly anyone at the table is looking at Jesus, in the left corner of the painting men in turbans appear to be climbing up the wall, left and right there is a staircase descending, a black boy in salmon-pink silk is pouring something from a jug, some of the men appear not to be joining in with the party, but the people in that palatial room are eating and drinking as if there is no tomorrow, you could almost forget this is a sacred moment that, two thousand years later, will still be repeated every day all over the world in every Holy Mass, and that was exactly what bothered the Inquisition, and so Veronese had to appear before the Holy Tribunal to explain himself. The painter does not seem too impressed, his answers are brief, laconic. They ask if he knows why he was summoned, and he says that he thinks so. He addresses them politely as "Most Illustrious Lordships", but seems to be pulling their legs a little. That dog, what is the dog doing there, a dog in the vicinity of Jesus, this is surely blasphemy? He should have painted Mary Magdalene there, should he not? Yes, but he did not think she would look right in that

spot. And that bloody nose? That's not fitting, is it? Yes, but it was intended as a servant who had had an accident. And what about that man there, the one who looks so German, armed with a halberd? That would take some time to explain. Please answer!

You see, we painters are accustomed to taking the same liberties as poets and madmen, and so I painted those two halberdiers, one eating and the other drinking at the foot of the stairs, yes, but so that they can immediately be of service, because I believe that a man as wealthy as the host would have had such servants.

And that fellow who looks like a court jester, with a parrot on his fist, what is he doing there?

He is there for decoration, as is customary.

And who is sitting at the Lord's table?

The twelve Apostles.

What is Saint Peter doing, the first one sitting there?

He is carving the lamb into portions for the whole table.

And the man beside him?

He is holding up his plate.

And the next one?

He is picking his teeth with a fork.

Who do you think was actually present?

I believe there was only Christ and his apostles, but if there is any space remaining in a painting then I fill it with figures of my own invention.

So did someone commission you to include Germans and jesters and people of that sort?

No, Sirs, but I saw that I had lots of space, so I could add a great deal.

The conversation continues like this for a while, and of course he has to confess that this is not a worthy company for such a holy event, as he already knows what the verdict will be: within three months the canvas must be painted over, the dog and the bloody nose and the tooth-picker, along with the Germans, must be removed – but the painter has already come up with a plan, with the permission of the Dominicans, who want to keep the painting as it is. He barely changes the painting at all, he just gives it a different name, and that is what it is still called today in the Accademia: *Feast in the House of Levi*, and if paintings were allowed to have a subtitle, in this case it might be: *or, Hoodwinking the Inquisition.*

Voices, Organ, Rain

THE STORY GOES THAT JUST ABOUT ALL VENETIANS LEAVE their sinking ship in the evening. Rents too high, too many tourists. They live in Mestre, or even further away in the Veneto. Maybe they lived here once, but left because of the children, because of work, because of old age. Now they never come, or just to work, real commuters. Waiters, carabinieri, teachers, nurses, the crews of the vaporetti. So I always feel as if the city rises a little out of the water in the evening, like when you step out of a traghetto. But then who are the people who may call themselves Venetians? The ones who really live here and are not foreigners or visitors? Real Venetians, who would not dream of leaving their liquid city, no matter what happens. You cannot start asking passers-by or shop staff, at most you can attempt to tell by some sign or other which are those increasingly rare creatures who have not allowed themselves to be driven away by the ever-changing hordes, by high prices or high water. They are the ones who do not stand still on every corner to study the map, who turn down a dark alleyway with complete confidence. Who go to Mass when the tourists are still asleep. An old man in a semi-dark, dusty café somewhere in Cannaregio, reading the Venetian pages of the *Gazzettino*. Old ladies at the Rialto market having entire conversations with the saleswomen, like good acquaintances. Women who do not stroll through the market but head straight for that one particular fish stall. If you come here long enough, you can try to recognise the signs, Venetian dialect, animated local discussions, a patient queue at a municipal office. How many of them are left? Tempered by centuries of experience and immune to the hundred people every day who ask the way, to Russian and English accents, resistant to invasion, clinging to a sense of togetherness, possessors of a secret doctrine that excludes the others, who recognise each other by a word, an expression, and know what is cheaper where, at which time it is better not to take the vaporetto, who should not be charged tourist prices, and where they can be among their own people, who know the codes and the secret laws of the city, and recognise the pseudo-Venetian at a hundred metres. It is their city, which once again becomes theirs when all those others have left, the eternal labyrinth through which only they know the way, the city whose burdens they bear as if they have been chosen.

I arrived at these thoughts by looking around in the church of San Rocco on Sunday, November 25, 2012. Only

Venetians, I thought. Outside, it was pouring down. In a local café where I had escaped the rain for a hot *cappuccio*, I had seen the small poster: "Musica e Spiritualità. A performance at the San Rocco, Coro Thomas Tallis di Arduino Pertile, Thomas Mazzucchi direttore. Francesco Bravo organo." It would begin at five o'clock and it was already getting on for five, it was actually already dark outside, I hurried through the rain showers to the church. The concert was free, and I found one of the last places inside. Palestrina and Palestrina, then three times Gregorian, a toccata by Gabrieli, William Byrd, Christopher Tye, all of a pleasantly old age. In the church, everyone seemed to know each other, people waved and peered at each other, kissed, shook hands, no doubt about it: this was an extremely Venetian affair, they were among their own, the music would lift us up, church and all, you could rely on Palestrina for that. At such moments, there is no mortality, Palestrina has been dead for more than four hundred years, the words from which he had composed his four-part song were written as a psalm a few thousand years ago and were about a river that then, as now, flowed near Baghdad. People had sat lamenting on the banks of that river, exiles in Babylon who had dreamed of Zion, I was in an old church in an even older city and because I knew the words and knew what they meant I too became unimaginably old, I was part of something, together with a few hundred people in wet raincoats I sat in a space that was protecting us from the gloom of the autumn weather. The singers, men and women, stood at the front of the church, and yet close enough to see their faces. They are in black, standing in a semi-circle, the formations change for the different pieces, sometimes four step towards us while the others remain behind, and then the sounds undulate towards one another as in a responsory. Polyphonic music, no instruments, for a moment that almost inaudible tuning of the voices, a sort of holy humming, *moommmm . . . , miemmm . . .* yes, that's good, a nod at each other, looking at the conductor who allows silence to reign for just a little longer, raises his hands in that fraction of a second when there is not yet any music, and then it happens, suddenly the church fills with composed sound, voices interweaving, chasing, supporting one another, people who do not need an instrument to make music, their bodies are their instruments, the voices fly up past the tall columns, seeking out the walls, drifting through the vaulting, until the whole church is made of music and we are rocked, in harmonies that promise things that do not exist, except for now, in this music. A Catalan ballad from the fourteenth century, but otherwise Latin, a *Laudate*, an *Ave verum*, I remember the words from my time at boarding school. Singing people are beautiful, the everyday has disappeared from their faces, even to themselves they have become different people, a polyphonic instrument that swaddles and cocoons us. After the songs, when the large organ booms out, the whole church vibrates, you can feel it in your bones as if you are part of the building yourself, and when it is silent again, and you hear the squalls of rain dashing against the high windows, it is like sailing in a ship full of music through a perilous night, but with no fear of disaster.

For a moment, on an autumn evening, I had been a Venetian in Venice, I had sat among people who had heard the same as me, who, like me, had briefly been lifted up out of their day. There are no instruments that can measure such a feeling. At the vaporetto stop I watched the needles of rain scratching lines in the dark water, as if notes were being written in the black water too. On board, I found a place to shelter from the rain on the rear deck. Lights shone behind the tall windows of the palazzi, and through the rain and the sound of the engine I could still hear the music.

The Liquid City

Kafka's hotel

ANYONE WHO TRAVELS OFTEN TO THE SAME CITY BUT has no house there becomes a collector of addresses. I was woken in the middle of the night by a dull, repeated syncopated thudding, as if someone were playing two different types of percussion. But it must be percussion for giants, as I imagine it is making the bed shake. Again and again, a crashing blow, like waves slamming into an island, which is of course the case. Venice is an island, the lagoon is a part of the sea, the sea is agitated and slams against the quay, its violence sending the boats that are moored there clashing into the posts and each other, I try to name those sounds, but I do not know them yet. I lie still for a while and listen. I have come from the south of Germany, where I spent two months in a very quiet region in a very quiet and remote house, and even though it lasts just a few seconds, that unusual sound from outside confuses me for a moment. I have not yet turned on the light, I try to remember where I am, to reconstruct the room I must have entered last night, but the dimensions of that room are a puzzle that I need to solve, while caught in the fundamental sound that is coming from outside. Yesterday I woke up somewhere else, if there was any sound at all it must have come from the woods around the house, this is different, it feels as if it comes from a long way off, as if it is calling me, it wants to force me to determine the place where I am, I have to imagine the room where I am situated, and not only the interior of that room, but also the exterior. I have not yet lost my memory, this whole process takes place in a couple of seconds, and then literally, the confused consciousness relocates itself, finding its orientation in the vague darkness, tentatively venturing out of the equally strange bed and wandering to where a long, vertical strip of light is falling through what appear to be high curtains. My feet register parquet, I have not switched on the light or opened the curtains, but long before I reach the window, my consciousness has caught up with me and told me what I would see, in that one second reality had merged with expectation and the rocking boats coincided with the sound that had woken me, and I felt the force of the water beating against the quay, the lagoon smacking onto the land and then retreating to attack again. I was in Venice.

The room I had seen only at night transformed into a room in the early Adriatic light, large and spacious, old-fashioned, armchair, desk, engraving, drawing of a floral arrangement, it could have been 1920 or 1899, but it was now, my umpteenth now in this liquid city. Gabrielli-Sandwirth is the name of the hotel, from outside it looks elegant, the colour of cinnamon, my room had three windows at the front with a balustrade of white columns. A friend had once, long ago, spent her wedding night here, and she would later tell me that Kafka had written his sad letter to Felice in this hotel, a letter that probably read as if it were the last. That same year he had sent her more than two hundred letters and cards, so the message in this letter must have come as a nasty surprise. He has, he writes, reached the conclusion that art and love do not go together, he fears that nothing would come of his work. He expresses it more clearly in his diary: "coitus as punishment for the happiness of being together. I shall isolate myself from everyone, living as ascetically as possible, more ascetically than a bachelor, that is the only way for me to endure marriage."

I do not know whether he had the same room, and I do not actually wish to know. The tone of that letter, written so long ago, curiously fits the sounds coming from outside, which penetrated my night's sleep. Not only is the light storm making the boats bang together, there are also men out there now driving new mooring posts into the mud. I stand watching a little vacantly from my small balustrade, see an enormous tree trunk slowly vanishing into the water of the lagoon, also watch later as that pole is planed down, becoming less and less like a tree, think about Felice and how the writer's hand writes the last word and, together with the other hand, folds the letter, and how two other hands later open that letter in another country to read a fateful message. The old poles that have been extracted from the mud like rotten teeth are now lying on a flat barge, they have served their time. The mud is the colour of death, which is out of keeping with the sun over the lagoon. I was to stay in this hotel for three days until I could move into the apartment around the corner, which I had rented for the coming weeks in a narrow street that opens onto the Riva degli Schiavoni, close to the Arsenale vaporetto stop, an area I know only as a walker, not as a resident. The difference is a dramatic one. When, in the days that followed, I stepped out of my house in Ramo Pescaria and headed right, I did not have to fear the mighty army of Chinese tourists advancing upon me across the bridges from San Marco, I had a house to hide in if it got too bad, I lived there. I had never felt so Venetian. I had already lived near Campo San Samuele, in a dark apartment in a curiously dilapidated palazzo close to the Giglio stop, at the Fondazione Cini's converted monastery on the island of San Giorgio Maggiore and in peculiar places in the labyrinth of other *sestieri* that I would not even be able to find again, but now, for the first time, I felt that I had arrived. Outside the door was a brass plate with six bells and the names that belonged to them, including that of my landlord, who was temporarily abroad, and probably also that of an elongated man I regularly saw pottering around in the hallway and in front of the door, he wore a very long brown coat and a cap in the same colour, a rather English-looking figure from a thriller, who seemed to be part of the furniture and greeted me in a friendly fashion. Sometimes I saw a mother with children who did not notice me as a result of my sudden invisibility, as I was made of air, which meant human contact had become impossible, and the other six names had no bodies attached or lived abroad. Although, from time to time, a woman appeared with a trolley full of merchandise through a mysterious door behind which there appeared to be a storage room. I saw the tourist trinkets from her trolley on the pavement of the Schiavoni during the daytime, without the woman, unless she had the ability to transform herself into a man by day. The brass nameplate meant that I was now called Fabbri, a name I liked very much. T.S. Eliot once dedicated a book to Ezra Pound with the accompanying line *Il miglior fabbro*, the better craftsman, I had now become the plural of that, and it could not get any better. The first evening I had also found a café with walls covered in posters of football clubs, and I had decided I would drink my coffee there every day, perhaps a reaction to all my previous visits, which had resulted in a serious addiction to museums. An English couple sat next to me, watching the silent television, the man had a bird-like face and followed the movements of the somewhat scantily clad singer, above the bar was a rack from which the glasses hung upside down, the mood was subdued, you could also eat there, besides the English people, who soon left, abandoning their red wine, there was a group whose members knew one another, a phenomenon I began to recognise in the weeks that followed, the café as a sanctuary for Venetians, where for once no obvious tourists came and so as a foreigner you immediately try to fade into the wallpaper, I am not here, I am in fact invisible, I am just having a quick drink, and I will mind my own business. Two quiet Japanese tourists sat some distance away, but otherwise it was just the extension of an eternal living room, and the wine was good. On subsequent days, the English people had disappeared and so had the Japanese, I tried to look like a chair and, judging by the reactions, I succeeded, even though I still had to pay.

I am used to living in other people's houses. The cuckoo lays its eggs in the nests of other birds. This thought has always had a certain appeal for me, the accompanying sense of alienation does not deter me, if only because such a period always comes to an end. With a few small symbols – a book, a stone, a shell – you can make a room familiar, but the strange thing about the apartment where I am now is that I keep losing my way, regularly making a wrong turn on my way to the kitchen or the bathroom, even though it is not very big. This makes my time inside seem like the days outside: in Venice too it is not difficult to lose your way, something to which, if I am not in a hurry, I do not actually object, perhaps because I consider it a perfect metaphor for life, just like getting lost in that apartment. Maybe it is because it is so breathtakingly packed. Old family portraits, countless books, architectural drawings (the owner is an architect, his bookshelves crammed with wonderful studies, including one about the brilliant work of Aldo Rossi), mirrors that show a deformed version of you because of a century's tarnishing, bowls, plants in big pots on high pedestals, I feel as if I am supposed to become someone else, or that I have to act in a play but have not yet learned my role. The family portraits look upon me as an intruder and keep their secrets to themselves, they are the sepia colours of days gone by. Simone, who shares my life, is not bothered by it. She observes and photographs the world outside. Her play is staged on the campiello. The house has a small terrace that, like the kitchen, looks out over the campiello, a public square onto which a few alleyways open. As there are houses on four sides, it has the atmosphere of a courtyard, but also of a theatre, complete with all the scenery. A few trees, a couple of oleanders, fixed features. Within a few days we had all the characters worked out, only we did not yet have a plot. A cook in a uniform who sometimes came

racing out of one of the alleyways with something that we could not quite make out and then ran back again. The elongated gentleman with the cap, whom we had not yet named. A fat lady in slippers who sought out the middle of the square to make telephone calls, long, apparently dramatic conversations with all the accompanying gestures; Italian gestures are simply different, you can recognise *opera buffa* in them, but also a line of reasoning that must have to do with logic and cuts the conversation with the invisible other person into chapters and assertions with a decisive downward gesture with the free hand. The finest of all these actors was a person who lived directly opposite, an old and powerful figure. Her movements were slow but divine. The first time we saw her she was coming outside with her cane. In front of her house there hung a number of wires that we had not noticed until then, and now she was trying to pull down one of those wires with her cane, so that she could hang her winter coat on it. It is through such details that you get to know a city. The first few times it did not work but at last she had hold of it. She clearly could not care less that it still took quite some time before the coat, which by then had become a character in its own right, was finally and delightfully hanging in place. This was about airing your coat and saying farewell to winter. A green shimmer had appeared on one of the trees in the corner, and in a city of stone that is an order. Other items of clothing followed in the subsequent days, and what she could not know was that she was helping us to become a part of the city. This involves long campaigns of conquest. You observe faces and are in turn observed. Some portrait or other is made of you, you too are in the play that no-one wrote, you are someone. A foreigner who mixes broken Italian with Spanish, but who can read the *Gazzettino* or maybe just pretends, who asks at the Cantina Antica Vigna if you could just come outside so that he can point out the *tramezzino* whose name he does not appear to know but then two days later can pronounce, a café the size of a closet. So that is where you find the others who are part of your new life, such as the two perky and perfectly attuned butchers from Macelleria Maso, who, knife in hand, can dissect the mysteries of the *bollito* like a philosophical problem and send you away with the solution and their blessing, the three old men from Alimentari Ortis who may well have been standing there since 1914 behind their hams and cheeses and the moist, oh-so-white gleam of the *stracchino* from the Dolomites, 33 per cent discount today!

It was as if around those few narrow streets a wall had been erected that separated us from the world of mass tourism that raged less than a couple of hundred metres away. When we remained within those walls or inside the apartment, it seemed as if that world was a bad dream, the only sign we sometimes saw was a group of Japanese people down below on the campiello three times a week, a place their guide had perhaps picked out because there was nothing to see and so no other tourists, and he could tell his apparently serious story about Venice in peace. He always stood under one of the trees, with them in a circle around him, they listened calmly, almost withdrawn, even when it rained they stood motionless beneath their umbrellas, the difference between that and the onrushing armies on the Riva and the compact, impenetrable crowd by the Bridge of Sighs, which you have to pass through on your way to Piazza San Marco, could not be greater. What we had found was one of those enclaves where the last Venetians are holding out until the tourists take over for ever. And then, as if you are being funnelled from one trap into the next, there is another square behind or to the side of our *campiello*, larger, more open. A café with tables outside, a small church opposite, a façade in three parts, brick, Gothic, low and therefore pleasant, I have often walked past it, it is San Giovanni in Bragora. The strange name intrigued me, I had looked up the word and not found it, but in the old Italian guide by Giulio Lorenzetti I had read that *bragora* comes from the local dialect and has something to do with either the fish market or with the fishing trade, but also with the Greek *agora*, which means open public space. There was no sign of fish at any rate. It is not hard to become weary of churches in Venice, there is an infinite number of them, and you are weary of churches when you no longer see what is special

or, even worse, when the special becomes ordinary. Big or small, the altar is always in the same place, there are crucifixes and Marys, confessionals and choir stalls, such a surplus of holiness that it turns against itself, at such times you are better off reading Ruskin, who dissected the city's buildings stone by stone, obsessively studied and named all the forms, up to and including elements of arches and frames, it is the best way to cure yourself of your superficiality, every part of an ornament has a name, after that you will never carelessly walk past something again. According to Ruskin, ornaments had to be *governed*, they should not be allowed to be in control, they had to serve. "Lose your authority over it, let it command you, or lead you, or dictate to you in any wise, and it is an offence, an incumbrance, and a dishonour. And it is always ready to do this; wild to get the bit in its teeth, and rush forth on its own devices." Why you go inside one time but not another is a mystery I do not wish to unlock today, but I do think back to Ruskin's wise lesson, look at the façade, notice that I am tracing the movements of the three arches of the *raccordi laterali* with my head, read in my Lorenzetti that relics of John the Baptist were brought to Venice when Pietro III Candiano was doge, so in the ninth century, I read that this was Vivaldi's church and I go inside, and at the same moment the world of outside disappears, dissolves. Some churches are holier than others, that is simply how it is. Sifted light, the absence of others, dimensions, silence, fatigue, the gaze attaches itself to an object, a detail in a painting, it is impossible to calculate, rationality holds no sway here, does not count. But what does? Above the high altar, a painting by Cima da Conegliano. I pretend for a moment that I am a person from Japan and that I do not understand the picture. What is happening up there? Inside an extremely elaborate frame that would take hours to describe, a half-naked man stands in a loincloth. I cannot see from his face that this is a solemn moment and yet that must be the case, as he is definitely the one standing in the centre. To his right are three women with wings, one has a red cloth, the other a blue one, perhaps they are his clothes. He is standing barefoot in the sand, with his back to the water. The shore of that water behind him has rather wild plants growing on it, further back I can see a man on a horse who seems to be paying no attention to what is going on, he appears to be on his way to a high hill and the castle even further away to which a sandy path leads. Behind a second building that looks like a palace or a church, there are blue mountains but you do not notice them, as your attention is distracted by a second man, whose long right arm is holding a dish above the head of the first man. If I were asked what is happening up there, I would say that John the Baptist is baptising Christ, while at the same time wondering who it was who baptised John and how he knows that the water in that bowl has the power to found a religion, but that question is perhaps theological nonsense. The women I mentioned are, of course, angels, who have folded their wings behind them and are watching the event in silence, and the bird that appears to be standing still in the clear blue sky above all of this and is leading a squadron of winged children's heads is, of course, the Holy Ghost. Both John and the angels are standing on the ground above Christ, and everything seems to be taking place in perfect silence. How long can you look at a painting for? The silence of what I see has transferred itself to the silence in the church. It is only when the first visitor enters that the enchantment is broken, but when I go back outside I know that I have taken some of that silence with me, which I can use later or on some journey or other or when writing, supplies, provisions, what we used to refer to as victuals.

Water people

You can debate for a long time about the shape of Venice, Valeria Luiselli's broken knee or the split prawn that another poet saw in the famous perspectival cityscape by Jacopo de' Barbari in the Museo Correr, but now that I am sitting in front of an enormous map of the lagoon, the form of the city is remarkable mainly for its smallness. Admittedly, the map is large and is not in fact about the clenched form that we call Venice, but about the lagoon that has protected the city over the centuries and now sometimes threatens it. For more than a thousand years no-one could attack Venice, marshes, shallows, unknown passages, sandbars, everything conspired with the city to make it unapproachable, and the longer you look at that map the stranger the city around you becomes, with all those churches and palazzi. How on earth was it possible in this muddy marshland for something to develop that was so compact, a sort of clenched fist in the middle of nothing? Knee, fist, prawn, once you have walked around for a couple of hours, these comparisons become ridiculous again, but on the map they continue to exist. White areas, blue shading, numbers that indicate shallows, everything indicates danger for the stranger who ventures too far. In the past months I have been reading John Julius Norwich's masterful book about the history of Venice, wars, sea battles, the slow colonisation of the Adriatic Sea, the struggle with the Dalmatian coast dwellers, the occupation of Greek islands, the constantly shifting relationship with Byzantium, the participation in the crusades, the physical destruction of the other empire's capital city, and the later revenge of Islam, a continuous series of victories and defeats in which the physical existence of that lagoon was ultimately always the secret weapon that Venice had at its disposal, until another form of warfare invalidated that defence and the last doge removed his peculiar headgear with the words, "I do not need this anymore."

Seamanship, nautical ingenuity, heroic courage and the shipyard of the Arsenale, where new and newer ships could always be built, a day at the Museo Navale is sufficient to make the point. I have wandered there for hours among banners and figureheads, ship models and grappling hooks, portraits of sea heroes and defunct flags and medals, looking at the peculiar machines and objects that people invented to kill each other, but also admiring the fish- and bird-shaped ships with which the Venetians were able to control the sea that surrounded them for centuries. It must have been an intimate relationship, a man in full regalia on a high and decorated ship with a turbulent bride of water – that is how the doge sailed out every year onto the sea in his *bucintoro* to affirm their covenant with his wedding ring. I find a very distant echo of this in the way the young man or woman who has to moor the vaporetto uses the rope at every stop, because this too is an alliance, a literal one. They are sturdy, fibrous ropes, straw-coloured, of a considerable thickness, they put loops in them, wrap them around a mooring point, make a knot, pull the ship to the side so everyone can get off and on. It is all routine, they probably do not even think about it and I see it as a kind of ballet, a series of elegant movements that betray a great familiarity with rope and ship, and with the ever-moving water, to which all Venetians are married. Sometimes, when I have been watching for a long time, I think or dream that I might be able to imitate them, but that

must be my imagination. If the boat makes a jolt, or if the distance or the height difference between the quay and the ship is a little on the large side, and you need to get off or on board, you as a passenger become part of that ballet yourself, as the sailor's arm comes to your rescue. Sway, movement, rocking, a flurry of snow, high water, rain beating down on the deck, wind blowing the waves' hair the wrong way, the movement of a ship, far too large, sailing past, the nervous turmoil of roaming water taxis, gondolas that must be respected in their stately pace, cargo boats full of street waste, and the big ferry to the mainland, which looks like a tall Viking ship, the congestion of several boats at once and the throttling of the engine at the mooring places, everything that sails together on the water at different speeds, all part of that big ballet that has been going on here day and night for centuries now, only the type of boats has changed, the essence has remained the same, the interaction between people and water, with the boats as an extension of those people, or vice versa. Venetians are city dwellers with a swell, water people, inhabitants of a sailing, amphibious city.

Names

THE NAMES ON THE MAP OF THE LAGOON MAKE YOU want to travel. Away for a while from the alleys and the crowds, the churches and the saints. Venice has a wall of water, and sometimes claustrophobia strikes, and I have to get out. Lago delle Tezze, Ponte della Musa, Fondo dei Sette Morti – these are the names that people have given to this wet world, there is nothing finer than whizzing across all that water on the deck of a vaporetto. The lake of the Tezze, the bridge of the Muse, the Depths of the Seven Dead, names are irresistible. I have decided that I want to go to Chioggia, only I do not know exactly how to get there, and I am not in the mood for asking questions. On the map, the long, narrow strip of the Lido is directly opposite the city, at the end of that strip is Alberoni, and beneath it is an even narrower and more elongated island with a place called Pellestrina, but there is no bridge between those two islands. On the Lido, the brief shock of cars and, as a side effect, the people there look different too. But there is also a bus with a sign saying

Pellestrina, a bus that does not seem to require a bridge. I have not yet stopped to consider how that could be, I simply sit down, first we drive for some way through the built-up area, passing the famous Hotel des Bains, where Harry Mulisch would spend a month every summer, in imitation of Thomas Mann. It looks sad: faded glory, boarded-up windows, opposite a deserted beach. Kafka, Mann, Mulisch, that is quite enough. We drive a few kilometres, but then I have to get out because everyone has to get out. The empty bus drives on, an unsolved puzzle. Still I do not want to ask questions and I go with a few other disembarked passengers to wait for the next bus, which they are clearly convinced will be along soon. Destination unknown. Then we will see what happens next. And, of course, like the others, I get onto the bus that comes, the ticket for the first bus appears to be valid on the second one. Now we drive onto a long strip of land, on the map it is almost entirely road. To the right, something that resembles marshland, to the left a kind of endless sandy beach with campsites where nothing is happening at this time of year. I sit on the right-hand side of the bus and see, further and further away, the silhouette of the city that appears to float on water, a vision of Venice. We drive to Alberoni and stop at a car park. Here, I do ask a question and I am directed to another bus, which, without warning, drives onto a ferry, now I am sailing and riding at the same time, but that is not true, of course, I am sailing in a

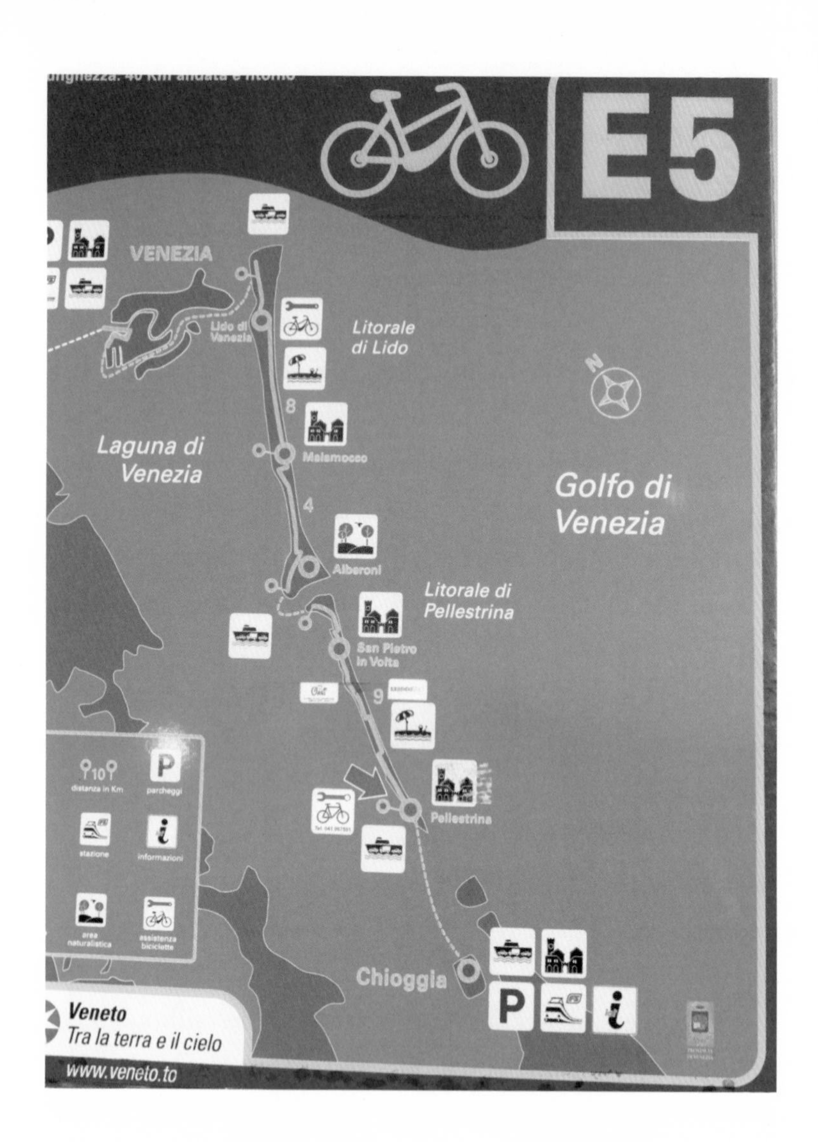
E5
VENEZIA
Lido di Venezia
Litorale di Lido
8
Laguna di Venezia
Malamocco
4
Golfo di Venezia
Alberoni
Litorale di Pellestrina
San Pietro in Volta
9
Pellestrina
Chioggia
distanza in Km
parcheggi
stazione
informazioni
area naturalistica
assistenza biciclette
Veneto
Tra la terra e il cielo
www.veneto.to

stationary bus to the next island, the even longer and narrower strip of Pellestrina, an increasingly thin line of sand, another road with waterworld on both sides. I still do not know how to get to Chioggia, but I have a firm faith, which is not disappointed because, at the end of this ride, there is a big boat waiting to sail to the harbour of Chioggia.

As I have read my Norwich, I know that the army of Pippin, son of Charlemagne and therefore King of Italy in Ravenna, wanted to go in the opposite direction from here in 810, over to where I have just come from, a first attempt to conquer Venice from these islands, exactly where today, on my bus and on a ferry, I crossed the Channel of Malamocco. In historic places, long ago is always a form of yesterday. The world politics of those days has become invisible, but still, you try to imagine what was going on in the lagoon. I have left the narrow strip of the island behind, the sea that must have looked the same as then, the few islands I came from today and which in those days were called Rialto and Olivolo and as a group were already ruled by a doge but only much later would become the Venice that we know now, all of them chess pieces in a battle between the old Roman Empire in the form of Byzantium, and the new Frankish Empire from the north, which penetrated far into Italy, with a divided Venice as a stumbling block between the two. The eastern empire of Byzantium was furious because the Venetians had gone to the coronation of Charlemagne on

Christmas Day in the year 800. But Venice itself was also split. Three brothers were doge at the same time – something that would later become impossible – and they asked Pippin to occupy Venice in order to confirm their rule, but when Pippin actually came, the Venetians forgot their infighting, temporarily shoved the doges aside as traitors and decided to defend themselves with the help of the lagoon, exactly at the point where today I crossed from Pellestrina to Malamocco. Every indication of navigation channels in the treacherous water was removed, passages were blocked with posts and rubbish, the marsh's banks of mud and sand and the constantly recurring high water took care of the rest, there was no way through. Malamocco is still on the island that is now called Lido, which, like the narrow strip of Pellestrina, blocked the access to Venice, so that Pippin could not set foot ashore in Malamocco either from Chioggia or from Pellestrina, but as a precaution women and children were sent to the island of Rialto.

A few weeks after being forced to admit defeat, Pippin was dead, and of course all this became a story in which the independent spirit of the Venetians had triumphed, a reputation that would stand the Republic in good stead in the centuries to come. To imagine it, I need nothing more than the water around me and the silhouette of Chioggia in front of us. But it is mainly the dimension of time that is on my mind: how and, above all, when did they know, so far over the Alps in Aachen, what was happening down here? How long did messages take to arrive? What was the role of rumours? Was it true that a Byzantine fleet would come to the islanders' assistance? This was a struggle for hegemony between two empires, the Frankish Empire of Charlemagne, and the Byzantine heirs of Rome in Asia Minor, who could not yet know that this would be the start of a thousand years of seafaring and combat, and certainly not that those few fragmented islands that were not yet a real city would join together to become a great naval power that would find its new fiefdoms on the other side of the Adriatic Sea and not to the west. History is a magician and a juggler who can keep all kinds of balls and clubs up in the air at once. The Pope had much of the Italian mainland under his control, making him a secular ruler, but also a spiritual leader, a dual role that, over future centuries, would regularly set him on a collision course with the northern city of water. In the few hundred years before Pippin tried to cross from Chioggia, a great deal had already happened, and that too is history, but a history that looked like marshy sandbars, islands, landing places for people who were fleeing the Lombards on the mainland, just as Libyans and Syrians are now fleeing the Islamic State. Immigration, mass migrations, but no-one lived on the islands back then except birds and crabs, yet another form of immigration. However, on the edges of the mainland and in the lagoon itself there was constant fighting, if only to determine what went with what and who went with whom. And, above all, who had authority over whom, and it is not long before colourful figures emerge in this world that has not yet been established, the exarch of Ravenna, the patriarch of Aquileia who could consider himself the successor of Saint Mark, and who, like the rest of the people in 568, fled from the Lombards and went to Grado, but there was already a bishop in that place, who had built his new and magnificent basilica among the Roman ruins.

As I sail for Chioggia in my fleeting today, I go back and back in time, into the turbulence of schism and war, everything that preceded Venice. They flee to Grado, a new bishopric is founded, the two patriarchs become rivals, a hellish battle breaks out between gentlemen who should have occupied themselves with the heavenly realm, a problem that is not solved until 1019 by uniting the two dioceses. What did the place we now know as Venice look like in those turbulent centuries? Like a plural. In those days they spoke about Venetiae, a number of islands scattered throughout a marshy area. After the battle with Pippin, it had become clear that Malamocco could never be the capital, the settlements on the various islands were no more than villages, tribunes and bishops fought each other in the lagoon, the Byzantine Empire, of which these parts were a province governed from Heraclea, began to disintegrate, many attempted insurrection, new leaders were chosen on the mainland, but also on the islands, and the first one chosen by the islanders was Ursus, not a lion but a bear, who, as Orso, which means bear in Italian, was to become the third doge of Venice, a title that for a thousand years would be carried by more than one hundred men in an uninterrupted succession of doges, until the last of them, Ludovico Manin, abdicated in 1797. Only ten years later, in 1807, Napoleon himself, who had said he would be an Attila to Venice, arrived in the city. Doge comes from *dux*, leader. Over a century later, someone else who had not read history properly would call himself *duce*, and the consequences of that are well known.

A gust of wind chases through the historical cobwebs around my head, blowing at Pippin and his army, at the patriarch of Grado, the Pope and the emperor of Byzantium, a moving and transparent tapestry that exists only for me. With the others, I have walked down the gangplank. I am back on land, and that is a peculiar sensation, because this land is mainland, now I am attached once more to the rest of the world, I could take a large detour and approach the island city from the other side, which says something about the conditioning you undergo in Venice. On the way here I have focused on history. I do not think everyone is bothered by it, it has something to do with my own character, the feeling that in these regions the air is saturated with history, a different sort of air with names and dates as atoms, charged particles that may be invisible to others but that have an odd effect on me, forcing me to look at inscriptions and monuments, wanting me to see traces of the past everywhere, an abnormality you can fully indulge in Venice, in part because you are not distracted by traffic. You walk, the pace of your feet is the rhythm, and already you are almost in an epic poem, you read the city together with the beat of your footsteps.

It is no different here, the sea is behind me, and what lies before me is a long, wide street that appears to run to the horizon, Chioggia. The accompanying feeling is one of paradox, and maybe that is because there is little traffic, as now that I am finally away from all that water, it seems as if that wide street is a river, and that I am walking on asphalt as if it is made of water. After a few weeks of Venice, I feel something falling away from me, something I have not felt to be a burden in the city itself, and yet a form of freedom and lightness, as if I have been released, relieved, and I walk past the big tower with the big clock that has been telling the time for all those centuries, and I go into the *pescheria* where the fish prove an existential point by looking exactly as they did in the days before that tall tower was built, a form of permanence with which no history book can compete. A Roman, a Greek, a soldier of Pippin or of Napoleon, all of

MANIN

them would recognise these fish, like a great silver treasure they lie there alongside all the shellfish, which, as they did back then, are hiding away in the stone fortresses they have built themselves. We are the ones who, throughout the course of time, have donned different clothes in order not to resemble our ancestors too closely. No-one would be able to say with any certainty whether the taste of those fish has changed in all those centuries, although we know there are now substances in the seas that were not there before. Two long rows of low shiny metal tables under a red tent, I stroll past them, people are already scrubbing away, the sunlight falls into the water, my gaze is briefly caught by crabs, eels, sardines, shells, but I know that it has filed away something else, and I turn around. Sometimes that happens, you have noticed something without seeing it or seen it without noticing it, and it is only when I have left that long red tent and turn around that I see it, a narrow gate of yellow bricks with a lavish array of sculpted reliefs of naked small and larger children in rectangular panels. I am not supposed to find it beautiful, since the explanation beside it says it is Fascist architecture. I should have seen that, of course, but what made me turn was something else. As in a *trompe-l'oeil*, feet and hands, sometimes arms and thighs too, have ended up outside the strict rectangles of the panels, which makes it look a little as if those bodies are moving. The text refers to the *stile razionalista e celebrativo dell'architettura fascista*, the rationalist and celebratory style of Fascist architecture, whatever that might mean in this context, but at the same time it mentions the influence of Donatello, and the story behind it is a simpler one. Originally there was not supposed to be a fish market here, but a school, and the sculptor, Amleto Sartori (Italians are bold enough to call their children Hamlet), was commissioned by the parents of a dead child to

make a monument depicting everything their daughter would never experience, dancing, playing, reading, and that is what these children are doing. Prisca was the name of that little girl who never played and never read, and in a hundred years' time, Prisca's gate will be beautiful, mark my words. There are forms of ugly innocence or contemporary kitsch that have to bide their time. Then the emotion will have won out over the Fascism.

A little later, back in the wide main street, I see proof of this above the entrance to a modern shop, in the form of the statue of a monk who is holding the two ends of his cord in his right and left hands, as if he is about to start skipping. I do not know who the sculptor was, as there is nothing written there. I estimate it as eighteenth century, and maybe it was not beautiful then either but still I stop in front of it. His body against the straight stone wall is moving a little too gracefully to one side, as if there is music playing somewhere and he wants to start dancing, left and right are two kneeling nuns. They are wearing Ku Klux Klan masks with eyeholes, their folded hands are raised towards the monk, a puzzle that I will not solve today. I walk out of the wide street to a low square gate that leads to a bridge from where I can see the lagoon again. On the back of the gate is the Venetian lion like an almost-Babylonian relief, its left paw on the open book, its wing stretched along its back, forehead wrinkled, tail curled, ready to descend and walk with me along the wide street to the boat. Imagination is the ability to dream in the daytime and to see what no-one else sees. Together, the lion and I walk along the street. When I stop at the Campanile of the duomo and try to estimate its height, my companion says, "Are you trying to count the bricks?", but you are not surprised when a lion says something in your dreams, so I pay no attention and read the words about the tower. It is from the eleventh century and was restored in 1312. The mayor then was Pietro Civran. So Pietro Civran has been dead for at least seven hundred years, but I have just read his name. I will forget it again, but that does not matter. Someone has wanted me to read his name, and I have done so. Anyone who does not believe that the dead still belong has failed to understand. On November 4, 1347, the tower collapses, a number of houses are destroyed by the rubble, an old woman dies but is given no name, and neither are the seventy-two men who are chosen at random from among the citizenry to clear up the mess. What those men said to one another about Civran has not been preserved. On November 14, after a solemn Holy Mass, the first stone is laid, and three years later the tower is finished for the second time. On the boat, no-one notices that a lion is sitting beside me, and by the time we have sailed to San Marco by way of the Lido, he has disappeared. He has left his newspaper behind.

Figures, fragments. Close to the Bridge of Sighs, on the banks on the narrow canal that enters the Bacino di San Marco there, I see something that is a cross between a well-functioning conveyor belt and a ballet. I stand to one side, and directly opposite I see a small group of Chinese people. They are not well-dressed Japanese, but rather people from the endless countryside, with age-old farming faces and the associated patience. It has started to rain gently. They are waiting for a gondola, and I am waiting too, only I am not waiting for a gondola but for what is going to happen. I know that it is anthropological curiosity that drives me, an insight into how globalisation works, or how two quite dissimilar civilisations with very different intentions collide. Compulsory enjoyment for one exchanged into necessary money for the other, a cliché as an unforgettable memory versus a conveyor belt of people, and therefore a living. Beside me there is a gondolier who is not rowing the gondola, but who is part of the team of three. His role is to help the Chinese people out of the boat, the two on the opposite side have to fill the boats again. But it is the man beside me who interests me. He has developed a fabulous technique, the lifting-old-Chinese-women-out-of-the-gondola technique. He holds out his left arm, and a little old lady's hand is placed on it, bearing the marks of a lifetime of hard work. Now he pulls her up, which naturally makes the boat rock. If she is afraid, you cannot see it. Then his left arm makes an arc and lifts her to the bank, but – and this is the miracle – at the same time he makes an arc in the air with his right arm, which ends in an outstretched hand with an outstretched finger imperiously pointing at a hat that is lying on a stool. It is where the tip must go. It is not exactly gentle, and because the old lady does not weigh much, it seems for a moment as if she is floating, but she lands safely, the man's left arm swings to the next in line, the right hand points. Meanwhile, the Chinese waiting on the opposite side get in and disappear into the iron light of the lagoon, a group of people pressed together, shrouded in drizzling rain. I see them looking up from below, out of the wobbling boat, at the man in the straw hat who rows standing up, as the narrow gondola vanishes across the choppy black water towards San Giorgio.

More anthropology. How little time does it take our brains to judge another person? How swiftly does the gaze of a Venetian register that I am a foreigner? The first row of every vaporetto is reserved for the elderly, this is clearly marked on the backrests, someone with a stick, that must be me, even though I have no stick. The problem is that if someone has unlawfully sat on such a seat, his or her back covers the unambiguous pictogram. But I have a certain expression, and if someone is sitting there who does not belong because of

their unseemly youth, then I use it. You must not say anything, because then you will instantly be unmasked. But they have an expression too, one that you can see every day. In shops, bars, at counters. That look is as fast as lightning, honed by centuries of experience. Within a second, you have been registered. This has always been a city for foreigners. The game is to make the uncertainty last a moment longer, to be a Venetian for a mini-second before the inevitable unmasking takes place. On the one hand, they live off us, on the other they are threatened by our masses and leave the city in the evening like a sinking ship. And how do you make it clear that you are not part of the mass? Do you disguise yourself with a *Gazzettino*? Dye your hair? The person who travels and wishes to write about what he sees does not want so much to belong as to be partially invisible. Invisibility is the best guarantee of observation. The metamorphosis into a pavement, into a church pew, a gravestone or a work of art is not simple. And yet, for more than forty years now, you have surrendered yourself to the city for shorter and longer periods, you have kept returning as if you had a right to it, but what right do you actually have? Brodsky, in his magnificent Venice book, *Watermark*, also mentions anthropology, but in relation to himself: "For all the time, blood, ink, money, and the rest that I shed or shelled out here, I never could convincingly claim, even to myself, that I'd acquired any local traits, that I'd become, in however minuscule a manner, a Venetian."

In spite of the fact that I was born in The Hague, and all my life have spent much of the year travelling abroad, I remain inalienably an Amsterdammer. This is something you cannot prove, it has to do with how much certainty you can enter an unfamiliar café as if you belong there. Even if it is a typical Amsterdam bar like a front room, you have the language as identification, and the paradox is that this does not apply to someone from Maastricht. You have lived for more than half a century in a city, your bed is there, your house and your books, even when you are not there, you are not a stranger. What Brodsky sees very clearly is that, no matter how often he returned to Venice, he always remained a traveller in transit, a passer-by who has not become a part of history, while, and this is what it is about, the city on the Adriatic has become an inalienable part of his life. I once wrote a book called *Voorbije passages* (Past Passages), a book about travelling as a way of life. You have stood on the banks of the lagoon, the movement of the water, always different, has penetrated your soul, you will never be rid of it, and the city and the water continue without you, your shadow has disappeared among the squares, the bridges, the churches and the palazzi, it is they who have written the words you thought you had written, but you were only the fleeting statue on a bridge or in a gondola, a temporary part of a city that for more than a thousand years has acted as if time does not exist.

Now that Amsterdam, too, has been overrun by hordes of

tourists, I understand even better what Venetians think, tourists, particularly when they walk along in lines following a flag, are a plague that must be endured, just like the abhorrently large boats in which they advance between Giudecca and Dorsoduro for their one divine day, when they will be able to spend all their time photographing what they will never see again. Between their gaze and the city there will always be a mobile phone or some other device that shows their own face with, behind them, the city they so wanted to see.

How does it work with statues in a city that has so many of them? I must have seen him often before, the tall, stern man in a bronze monk's habit, but I had not yet really noticed him. He stands on a high pedestal close to the Santa Fosca on Strada Nova, and it seems I have always taken him for granted, never looking to see who he actually was. A nation of statues lives in Venice, I always think they visit one another at night to talk about their lonely fate, but because they never come down from their pedestals in the daytime and you never encounter them at eye level, you keep on seeing them as part of the scenery, and therefore not really seeing them. Then there is the fact that his statue is set back a little, so that you have to walk over to it to see who this is. Paolo Sarpi. You cannot usually work out later why you walked to the statue that one time to see whose name was written there. I had noted the name in my book and had forgotten it again when, in a small antiquarian bookshop, I spotted an extremely small parchment book. Some books call you. I am not a real bibliophile or collector, but such a beautifully bound book, smaller than a hand so that it lies neatly on your palm with the colour of gleaming human skin, is something I find hard to resist. The beautifully typeset text – Venice had the best printers in the world – was in Italian, but not the Italian of the *Gazzettino*. This was about theology, I knew at once that I would never really be able to read it, I saw the name I had seen on that statue. Now a connection had developed between a tall, stern figure in a monk's habit and an extremely small book about a monk who apparently – that much I did understand – had fallen out with the Pope, and I also knew that this gem would travel with me to Amsterdam. The bookseller asked if I had a particular interest in Sarpi, because, if so, he had something else for me. I told him that Sarpi was still a closed book to me, but antiquarian booksellers are accustomed to stranger things. Booklovers fall into the category of peculiar people, and as printed books die out they will become even more peculiar. One comes in because he is missing something, another because of a special illustration, and here was a foreigner who loved small books. There are those days when everything falls into place, because a little later I was standing with another book about the same monk in my hands, this time in English. It was a beautiful book too, but not in a comparable way, a few centuries younger, but still, from 1894, with a cover of bright-green linen stamped with the golden emblem of Venice. I ran my fingertips over the lion's wings, read the name of the author, written in equally gold letters: Reverend Alex Robertson. The "ander" of Alexander should have followed the "x", but there was just a small golden "r" there now, with a golden dot beneath that miniature "r", which made the book impossible for me to resist. The small book was the older of the two and therefore the more expensive; as a reward, I got the other for a reasonable price. It bore the names of two previous English owners on the endpapers, the first of whom had bought it in Venice in 1896, while the second, judging by the more modern handwriting, had much later taken it to Sevenoaks in Kent, and an hour later I had already put my signature in it, and if everything happens as it should, then later it will be joined by the name of someone we do not yet know and who may well not have been born yet. As books become older, they perish less easily. At home I placed Robertson neatly with my Venice books, but when I began to study the small book more closely, something curious happened. Venice had the best printers in the world, I have claimed above, but when I unpacked the small book in my hotel room, something resembling a blush must have appeared on my cheeks. The book had not been printed in Venice at all, but in Leiden, in the Netherlands. It was written clearly: *Printed in Leiden, 1646*. I also found a description, very thinly folded: *Micanzio Fulgentio (attributed): Vita del Padre Poalo [sic], del Ordine dei Servi; Theologo della Serenissima Republ. di Venezia. 12.5 × 7 cm, 2 blank + title page with wood engraved vignette (Ae/ter/ni/tas)*. In very fine handwriting, it said in Latin that the book had been written by this Fulgentio: *Vita haec scripta fuit a Fulgentio & in Angliam Galliamque linguam translata est* . . . and also translated into English and French, but otherwise all three hundred pages were in Italian, with a number of pages at the back, concluding with a catalogue of the treatises of Paolo Sarpi and a sentence about the Inquisition and about Leonardo Donato, the doge of Venice.

In the days that followed I studied Fra Paolo Sarpi, as seen through the Presbyterian eyes of the Reverend Robertson. A friar of the Servite Order, founded in 1233, as the enemy of a pope, grist to the mill of a man who, since Henry the Eighth's reformatory revolution, no longer had to listen to the Pope in Rome. What soon became clear is that the Pope did not want to listen to this troublesome friar either, and subsequently tried for years first to silence him and eventually to have him killed. That this enmity was persistent is evident from the fact that Sarpi's name is not mentioned in texts about the order on the Internet. The Pope in question was Paul V, Camillo Borghese, one of those who ended up on the throne more or less by accident. His predecessor,

Leo XI, had died after just twenty-six days, the laborious and extremely political game of papal selection had to begin all over again, the various factions and families could not agree, and so it ended up being someone no-one had expected, or, as the Reverend Robertson puts it: "Paul V was a make-shift pope." Makeshift: a remedy, says my dictionary, but he did not remedy much, and if you want to know why, then you must look again at the portrait of Sarpi. Deep, almost black eyes looking out from a face that is stern and white, the face of a thinker, an astute lawyer, scientist, mathematician, the discoverer of blood circulation even before Harvey, and a friend of Galileo, for whom he ordered telescopes from Huygens in the Netherlands. But also, as a "theological advisor" of the Republic of Venice, a formidable opponent in the numerous conflicts with the ecclesiastical State, and as a counsellor of Venice a spider in the European web, which was sufficient to make Paul V suspicious of him and, later, hate him. The relationship between Venice and this Pope, still a cardinal at the time, was already tense, since he had once said during a conversation with the Republic's ambassador at the Vatican "If I were Pope, I would place Venice under interdict and excommunication", to which the ambassador had replied: "And if I were Doge, I would trample your interdict and excommunication under foot." When, in 1605, he did indeed become Pope, the conflict could have begun in all earnest, but for the fact that the new Pope was not only religious but also superstitious. In Subiaco, about fifty kilometres from Rome, there was a sweating Madonna who, when she broke out in sweat, predicted the death of a pope. A Flemish astrologer had also said that Clement VIII would be succeeded first by a Leo and then by a Paul. And the same Church that would not allow Galileo to say that the Earth orbited the sun believed that if Leo had died so soon after Clement, then Paul would suffer the same fate, but when months had passed and that prediction did not come to pass and stargazers had declared that the danger was over, the fight between Venice and Paul V could begin. For the Vatican, there were plenty enough reasons, as the Republic of Venice had decided that no new churches or monasteries could be built there without permission. Old Venetian laws about the ownership of land and buildings once more came into force, the separation of Church and State was rigorously applied, not only in the city, but in the surrounding areas, and that was quite significant at a time when more than half the city consisted of buildings and gardens that were the property of the Church. There was also another conflict: about who had the right to prosecute priests, the Republic or the Church, and Paolo Sarpi acted as a particularly sharp opponent of the Pope in this regard. The case itself was an opera within an opera. Two priests (one of whom, it later turned out, had never been ordained) had flagrantly misbehaved, one had constantly tried to seduce his niece and, when that had failed, had smeared her door with faeces, whereas the second had gone even further, as the words rape and murder are mentioned in the documents related to the case, whereupon the Council of Ten, the city's highest governing body, decided to start an investigation, to have the two men arrested and tried, a privilege the Church claimed for itself. Robertson had the space to write an entire book about it, the excommunication from Rome was indeed forthcoming, no-one was allowed to take confession, no-one was allowed to celebrate Mass, and no-one in Venice paid any attention. An excommunication of a city that is actually a state had never occurred in Europe before, and in various capital cities, rulers held their breath.

But a number of things happened before then. Venice was not at all keen on the Vatican's Spanish-friendly attitude regarding Spain's fight against the Protestant uprising in the Netherlands, so there was also conflict within foreign policy. And in Italy itself, the Pope had gained power over Ferrara, which meant he had come very close, which also caused Doge Grimani great concern. Venice was an important player in the Europe of that time, and the city had at its disposal a state theologian and adviser, as his title had it, in the battle against Rome, in the person of Sarpi the friar, and one with which the Pope and the curia could not compete. The city had been excommunicated and simply went on with its life, and because Venice and Sarpi had won that battle and the

ensuing battles, that statue is still standing on Strada Nuova. A reformatory wind seemed to be blowing from the lagoon. Sarpi did not mince his words in his letter to the Church, and the Pope smelled a heretic. That this heretic was a friar who was admired by Sir Henry Wotton, the British ambassador in Venice, shows the European scope of this game. As an expert in canonical law, Sarpi knew how to choose his words. Through a "divine law that cannot be undone by any human power, Princes have the authority to make laws within their jurisdictions that are related to temporal and worldly affairs: there is no reason for Your Holiness' admonitions, as the matters in question are not spiritual but worldly."

The term he used was "temporal" but in those days that meant "of this world". The message hit hard, and on April 16, 1605, the Pope announced that if Venice did not bow, excommunication would follow. The city's answer followed on May 6. The new doge, Leonardo Donà, announced that in the affairs of this world he recognised no authority higher than the divine majesty himself. The rest of the message is along the same lines, Venice will not listen and tells the clergy of the city to continue caring for souls and celebrating Masses, as the Republic's absolute intention is to continue in the holy catholic and apostolic faith and to adhere to the teachings of the Holy Roman Church. Subsequently, on Sarpi's advice, the doge orders the expulsion from the city of the Jesuits who, as John Julius Norwich recounts, were inclined towards the Pope because of their Spanish orientation. They want to leave the city on their own initiative, in a solemn procession that everyone can see, but are instead taken from their beds at night, so their propaganda trick fails. This would be another fine scene for an opera. All in all, the whole affair, news of which spread like wildfire throughout Europe, was a defeat for the Pope and the curia. The excommunication was lifted in 1607, but the Pope was still not finished with the friar. In his *History of Venice*, Norwich gives a less subjective account than the anti-papal Robertson. He relates that Paolo Sarpi remained calm in the midst of all the controversy, reiterating and reformulating the issue. "To some he was an Archangel; to others, Antichrist. In Venice, people prostrated themselves to kiss his feet; in Rome and Madrid, his writings were publicly burned. Inevitably, he was cited before the Inquisition; predictably, he refused to appear." In Europe, Holland and England offered support, France did not dare to speak out clearly, but Venice knew Henry IV was on their side. All this called for revenge, at which point I return to the wonderfully partisan Robertson, and to the *opera buffa* with near-fatal consequences. I would have liked to see the conversation on stage, preferably sung, between Paolo Sarpi and a sort of papal envoy, the German scholar Gasparus Scioppius, who had renounced Protestantism, and now "as is commonly the case with such perverts" had become a "rabid Papist". This Scioppius was on his way to German princes in order to attempt to bring them back to the mother church, and he paused in Venice to mediate between Sarpi and the offended Pope. The Pope had a long arm, he sings, and had only allowed him to live so that he could take him alive. Sarpi sings back that he is not afraid of death, and that he does not believe that the Pope is capable of such dastardly behaviour. He was wrong about that, because on September 29, 1607, the "ever-watchful" ambassador of Venice reports to the Holy See about a plot against Sarpi. The Duke of Orsini's palace was teeming with criminals and assassins, including an unfrocked friar who claimed that the Papal Court had hired him for 8,000 crowns to kidnap or kill Paolo Sarpi. A letter of safe conduct through the papal territories and a guaranteed pardon were part of the deal. The Senate of Venice tracked down the former friar and his accomplices in Ferrara, and arrested them as they were leaving the city. They ended up in the same jail where Casanova would one day be imprisoned, the Piombi.

After that, nothing more was heard of them, but the doge and Senate had been warned, and they made sure that Sarpi never again wandered the narrow alleyways of the Venetian labyrinth alone, as it would be so easy to stab someone there. But as in a real adventure novel, it happened anyway. It is October 5, a misty autumn evening, when Paolo Sarpi sets off from the Doge's Palace, through the bustling Merceria, to his quiet cell in the Servite Monastery. A fire had broken out somewhere in the city, so he did not have his usual escort.

He was not entirely alone either, his servant was with him, and also an elderly patrician, Alessandro Malipiero, one of those old Venetian names you keep coming across. The three of them had walked through the streets of the Rialto, busy even in those days, and then along the alleyways of the neighbourhood behind it, scarcely wider than a person, and had come to the peaceful Campo Santa Fosca, where the statue now stands that led me to this entire story. Behind the campo are Rio dei Servi and Rio Santa Fosca, and across that water is a bridge, Ponte della Pugna, where (Robertson writes in 1890) wrestling contests used to take place. Now they are close to the Servite Monastery, and as they walk, one by one, across the bridge, five men come towards them, overpowering the servant and the aged patrician, and the leader sets about stabbing Paolo Sarpi's head and neck in a mad fury and then, as Robertson puts it, they left him for dead. But he was not dead. The Senate summoned physicians from everywhere, including from outside the city. The friar had been stabbed fifteen times with a stiletto, as they could tell from the holes in his cap, hood and collar. Only three of those blows had hit their target, however, two in his neck and one in his face, which had gone in through his right temple and come out between his nose and cheek, leaving him with a scar he would bear for the rest of his life. As the stiletto had bent with the force of the blow, the attacker had been unable to withdraw it from the wound.

*

After reading this, I walked back one late afternoon to Campo Santa Fosca to see the bridge where it all happened. The Servite Monastery no longer exists, it was destroyed in 1812, all I found by Rio dei Servi was the ruin of an old Gothic gate, the last remnant. There was no name on the bridge, and there is only one bridge from the campo towards where the monastery must have been. It was quiet when I was there. I stood on the only bridge I believe it could have been, which leads to Calle Zancani, which takes you to Campo San Marziale, where the church dedicated to that saint stands. I did not want to go any further. Whether it was that bridge or not, only a Venetian expert can tell me. If you then walk back to Campo Santa Fosca, Fondamenta Vendramin is on your left. I stood there for a while and thought to myself that with the autumn air – because it was autumn for me too – I was also breathing in the atoms of Venetian history, invisible as always. Where does everything go? Cries, knife stabs, papal intrigues, nothing remains, does it? The church that now stands on Campo Santa Fosca is no longer the same one as back then, it was not built until 1741. A dark Tintoretto hangs above a mourning Byzantine Mary with son. Tintoretto, Sarpi, did they know each other? The legal eagle and the man for whom hundreds of metres of canvas were not enough to paint his visions of heaven and hell. Did they meet in the narrow alleyways? They were partial contemporaries, and both were famous. All Venice is an eternal cross-reference, there is no escaping it, perhaps simply because you do not wish to. A city like a compact universe offers its own variety of claustrophobia, a domain that is enclosed and yet connected to the world. Maybe this is only a preoccupation of the later visitor. At the long peak of its history, Venice was a conqueror, a coloniser that not only discovered the world but also brought it back home, and at the same time it remained a domain surrounded and pro-tected by the sea, a contrast that the twenty-first-century visitor must try to reconcile in order to understand the city better. Which Venice is he visiting now, the one of greatness or only what remains? Is he going to leave it at the beauty of the museums or will he also attempt to penetrate to the soul of the city? The mercantile spirit, the urge for conquest, the rivalry that built everything he sees around him? As I stand again in front of the statue, none of this seems to trouble Paolo Sarpi. I have wandered back to his statue from the dark Tintoretto in the church next door and am among the pedestrians who are leaving the city after a day at work, on their way to the station. He stands there in the early Venetian evening, looking right through the stranger, who, for his part, in turn is trying to see whether or not the sculp-tor applied those wounds to the stern friar's face, but the growing darkness makes it difficult to see. I can understand why the Church, who had to revise her opinion about his friend Galileo, never declared this opponent, who, in spite of everything, did not wish to leave the Church, a saint, even though he was holy enough. A pope's revenge can last a long time, and can it seems be handed down to a later pope. Paolo Sarpi was not even granted a real place of rest, his grave being emptied on several occasions through the intervention of Rome, until finally he ended up in the church on San Michele. I did not wish to find out if he is still lying there. I am satisfied with his statue and that small parchment-bound book, found in the city where stories never end.

On the Trail of the Painters

HOW MANY PEOPLE CAN FIT INTO A PAINTING? AGAIN a year has gone by, and again I have returned, this time to follow an old trail, the books and notes I had brought from the previous time, pictures by Carpaccio, Bellini, Tintoretto. This city never stops, not in your imagination and not in reality. A city surrounded by water has no borders – it is everywhere. A city like a spider's web, the maze that you never get used to, you remain entangled in it, even when you have been away for a year. And the painters are part of the hide-and-seek, they are everywhere, but where are they? In the Frari, in the Accademia, the Madonna dell'Orto, the Scuola San Rocco, the Doge's Palace, they become a part of your eternal circuit.

And again I am living somewhere else, a quiet corner of the city that I did not yet know, a low house in a narrow alleyway next to a ruin that is being rebuilt behind black tarpaulin, the bedroom is at the height of the water, at night I hear the footsteps in that alleyway as if people are walking past my bed, when there are more of them I hear their voices like voices in a dream, full of half secrets. The question with which this story begins is hanging on the door, it is the reproduction of a painting by Tintoretto in which there are so many people and angels that I have hung it up there to look at for hours.

It is for that painting that I have returned, but also for the silence of Bellini and Vivarini, for the imagination of Carpaccio and Cima da Conegliano, but particularly because of the abundance of humans in Tintoretto, the painter you cannot miss in this city of human abundance. It is strange: the crowds I try to avoid during the daytime are precisely what I look for in Tintoretto. But I must begin at the beginning, even though after all these years there is never a beginning, there is only the repetition of beginnings. I have come across the Alps, via the Dolomites, past Bressanone, which is called Brixen up there, I still have the north with me, I came by car, in itself a rite of initiation: the driver who comes along the road to Venice must undergo a series of humiliations in order to become a member of this order. The wide motorway narrows, the speed is taken away from you, you pay a toll for the last time, you watch the train beside you going much faster, the city is now both near and far, you can already see the water like a promise to your right, but you have to go and queue in the only square where you can still drive, after a while you enter a dark garage, as if inside a snail's shell you spiral upwards, one, two, three, four floors, a man imperiously points out a spot among all the other humanless cars, you haul your suitcases of clothes and books – always too many books – out of the car to the lift, which is far too small, and then drag them further outside across Piazzale Roma. Not well thought out, this time, a bridge with lots of steps, then a long quay beside a narrow canal, another bridge, even narrower and higher this time, no beautiful houses, everything rather shabby, a dead church, another bridge, someone helps me, a narrow alleyway, a key, a house. A narrow stairway up, a room to the left of the stairs, two beds, a door to the outside, and when I open it, a small neglected patch of grass, a long wire with other people's clothes, a dead bush, a neglected brick wall with the remains of three chimneys, which later I will see again in an etching by a previous resident, and the rest of the view is made up of a dead church across the water. A lifetime of travelling has taught you that nothing is as bad as it seems at first, that every curious space you have ever spent time in will become part of your own inner landscape, absurdly I think now about a white stone room, just a few square metres, once on the banks of the Ganges, and then about the dingy room in St Petersburg where the student Raskolnikov plotted murder, and about what you once wrote yourself about how, like a cat, the traveller explores the new space of a hotel room with extreme wariness and caution, and that is what I am doing now. Such an exploration is always focused on one thing: Can I work here? Can I read here? How is the light? At that moment a hammering begins behind the wall beside me and I remember the scaffolding I saw outside.

My friends who had found this place for me had told me nothing about renovation. For a moment I stand still, then the hammering stops. The beds are very low, I lie on one and pretend to sleep, just to try it out. Sounds in Venice are different from those in every other city, as the absence of cars is also a sound, a sound in the form of silence in which you hear other sounds, as I can now. Footsteps, a voice walking past and talking almost to the rhythm of those footsteps, someone telephoning, a stray sentence wanders in and then follows the steps as they move away. The sentence, which should actually have been in a novel, reverberates for a while, and then the hammering begins again, and other voices, not Italian but Romanian, the labourers who are working on the house next door. I put my suitcases in a corner and head upstairs. When I open the shutters, I see the house across the street and know that if the neighbour extends his arm and I do the same, we will be able to shake hands. Calle de la Madonna, but not the one I know from before, this is a different one, an alley only two arms wide, but without a canal, in a part of town that is so much poorer and quieter. Upstairs, a sofa, a table, a dresser, drawings, watercolours. In one of them, I see the three chimneys I noticed outside. When I open the windows at the back I look out on the neglected lawn below, the dark water of a narrow channel with a cargo boat and, beyond it, the dead church on the other side of the water. By "dead", I mean closed for ever, empty windows, high walls of pink brick, Mass will never be celebrated there again. I haul the suitcase of books upstairs, put my computer on the table, place the books in the order I intend to read them. I am back. I open up the map on the large wooden table and search in the drawn labyrinth for where exactly the house is, where the nearest vaporetto stops are, and note that the area is called Santa Croce, that the church opposite is the Santa Maria Maggiore and that it is next to the Carceri. Later I learn that this is a women's prison and that my temporary landlord is an Italian physicist who has worked for years in California and now works as a volunteer at the prison, teaching what he calls "the girls". I also know now that I walked with my suitcases along Fondamenta Rizzi, the nearest vaporetto stop is Piazzale Roma or San Basilio, right at the end of the Zattere. This corner of Venice is another new book that I must learn to read, the map must turn into stone, only then can I start walking. San Basilio is opposite the tip of Giudecca, the stops on the other side are Palanca, Redentore, Zitelle. Close to San Basilio, there is a supermarket, where I can become Venetian again, as is only possible at markets and in shops. In the other direction is Campo Santa Margherita with the two fishmongers' stalls, but if I want to go to the real market and to the fish market, I will have to go by way of Piazzale Roma or through all the piazzas and alleyways to the Rialto.

Why have I returned for the umpteenth time? What is, in fact, the attraction? There are only fifty-five thousand Venetians still living in this city, the rest flee at the end of the day because their city is no longer their city, because the houses have become too expensive, because the way through the labyrinth is blocked at certain hours by clots of foreigners. So why did I come back? The first answer would be because I have not yet finished Venice, but that is nonsense, no-one ever finishes it, not even if you stay there your whole life. The past is a dimension of the present, as I read in Jorge Carrión's wonderful *Barcelona: el libro de los pasajes*, and when I walk around here in the present I am simultaneously in that other dimension. Could that be it? Am I living backwards, against the flow of time? In a city like this, you are surrounded by dead people who have left something behind, palazzi, bridges, paintings, pictures, the air is saturated with them.

Where does it come from, the extraordinary elation I feel here, ever since that first time, in 1964, more than fifty years ago now? Everything here was built by people, and yet it is as if the city *came into being*, built itself, and maybe even dreamed up the people who built it. An expanse of water into which a few rivers flow, almost a marsh, with islands in it here and there, people who were seeking refuge, and who built a city that has in turn produced this sort of people, a mutual creation through which something developed that exists nowhere else in the world, people who make a city that makes people who for centuries subjugate everything around them, a wondrous multiplication of power and money around a Church that never knew for sure whether it belonged to the East or the West, an excrescence in which the most unimaginable absurdities and traditions flourish, with the weirdest and most wonderful flower of all, that peculiar creature the doge, an immense series of men, the earliest of whom have vanished into the mists of history and the last of whom took that headwear, a piece of fabric that was a cross between a Phrygian nightcap and a crown, and removed it from his own head.

Have I gone astray? Not really. I began with Tintoretto and his crowds, which I know from San Pietro, San Giorgio, the Scuola San Rocco, from Santa Madonna dell'Orto. Tintoretto was not a medieval man, in his day the Santa Madonna must have been a building from the past, it does not always follow that those who come later will find what went before beautiful. Voltaire hated Notre Dame, he thought it a dreadful building. Santa Madonna dell'Orto is one of the oldest churches in the city, and because I have just arrived, I want to go there, not only because Tintoretto is buried there, and not because he made some of his gigantic wall paintings there either, but because I feel that this church lies at the back of the city, where it opens up towards Murano and Torcello, and mainly because it is a building of austere simplicity compared to the profusion of Renaissance and Baroque in so many other churches. It is always quiet and peaceful there, an open square, a Gothic brick building that looks narrow and high and does not reveal how much space there is inside. I like to sit in that square, there is a bench where you can read. You walk over Campo Largo and Campo dei Mori, cross Rio Madonna, and then you are there. On the corner you will have seen the three eastern-looking figures who are called the three Moors, who are not Moors but the three Mastelli brothers, who came to Venice from Morea in 1112. Immortalised by a misunderstanding, you go with your brothers to Venice, and eight hundred years later you have turned to marble and the three of you stand side by side on a façade.

I do not go inside yet, the church is still closed, I go for a walk towards the lagoon, see the sparkle of the water, rowers, the number 5.1 boat making its eternal circuit around the city. In this neighbourhood, which lies between the church and the lagoon behind it, there are humble residential blocks, a simple suburb of the kind you can find in any Italian city. The history that reigns throughout the rest of the city is suddenly far away. This is where the people must live who operate the machinery of Venice, the clockwork that keeps a city ticking, the workers on the vaporetti, hotel staff, nurses, teachers, who can say? Everything in this city is so spectacular that I have to go to the advertising pages of the *Gazzettino* to taste some normality, people offering something for sale, the invisible aspects of daily life as a counterbalance to the extreme visibility of everything. No bars here, no tables out on the street, just blocks of houses, the white light of a television screen in a dark room, turn the corner three times and you find yourself on the water and see the horizon of the distant mainland and the boats sailing to the islands.

There is no-one else inside the church. My guide is a paper one, from 1956, I found it years ago on the book boat, it once belonged to Paolo Barbini, always a form of unwanted intimacy, someone else's book. Is he still alive, this Barbini? Did he sell his book, or forget it somewhere? We do not know each other, and yet for years he has accompanied me on all my trips to Venice. The only problem is that guides know so much. This one was written by Giulio Lorenzetti, and he skips not one church and not one painting, and this alone tells me how selectively we look, or – to put it another way – how much we do not see or do not want to see. This is perhaps the tenth time in all these years that I have been inside this church, and I know why I keep coming back. Lorenzetti whispers about the visible transition here from Romanesque to Gothic, after which he works his way around

all the walls according to a military plan, I feel that I should follow him, but I have never been able to look in that manner. In a room to the side of the actual church is the statue of Mary that, according to legend, was found in a vegetable garden in 1377 and after which the church is named, the Holy Madonna of the Garden, but that is not what I have come for either. The story makes you think that the statue was under the earth, so that is what it looks like, a goddess of a mysterious sect, but what I have really come here for is to answer the irreverent question with which I began this chapter, how many people can fit into a painting, which is an awkward way of expressing wonder and admiration for Tintoretto's immense painting, *The Last Judgment*, to the right of the main altar, so large that you have to keep changing position in order to really see it. Death and damnation below, skulls on bodies that are still alive, a crowd crushed together, people who appear to be hanging over an abyss, dragged along naked in a torrent, a black man whose darkness stands out against the bewildered white face of a child behind his shoulder, winged creatures that seem to be whizzing through the air, bodies twisted in fear, a hundred years earlier no-one could draw a body like that, a new kind of human has emerged here, only to be destroyed, it is unimaginable that one single person made this, he has left room in all kinds of places in this apocalyptically swirling movement for a glimpse of open sky with luminous masses of clouds, the noise that must be going on up there is inconceivable in the silence of the church, you hear it without hearing anything. The eye wants to move upwards, away from the doom below, it has to fight its way up between backs and muscled arms, between half-naked people on red clouds and demonic visions of punishment and fear, to where it is finally brighter, to the unearthly glow of the circle of light above something that resembles a mountain top, where Christ is sitting with his face turned away, his left hand reaching for a floating sword that he does not grasp. He has turned his head towards his mother, who is sitting a little below him, above her a branch with a lily, also floating. It is as if they have nothing to do with that unbridled chaos so far below, this is the Last Judgment, but it seems as if it does not concern him. The figures closest to them are looking at them or at that blue-rimmed circle of light above, a woman with two children in her arms, a man with a palm branch, a man leaning against a cross, as if they too do not wish to see the horrors and the threat below. Someone can undoubtedly explain all of this, looking up has made me dizzy, and even though I have remained standing down below I have the feeling that I have climbed down from a great height. I know there are another two paintings here by him that are the same size, but instead I walk on, in front of the altar, to the side chapel, where the man who painted this is buried with his son and daughter. It is a very simple grave, a stone embedded in the wall. He lived nearby, Tintoretto, and then it really does become inconceivable, a man leaving his house and walking alongside the water to go to work here, he passes houses and people, with in his head the dimensions of a Last Judgment, a mathematical space that he has divided into lines that are still invisible to others in order to turn the images in his mind into images on a wall, to transform imagined colours into real colours, to tell a story that had occupied humankind for hundreds of years. How many people did he meet as he went to his work? If you could see all the human figures in all the Tintorettos that have been preserved in this city together in a piazza, you would see an immense crowd, an absurd thought, and yet one that imposes itself on me a few days later in the Gallerie dell'Accademia, when I am looking, as closely as I can, at the *Miracle of Saint Mark*, in which the saint frees a slave. Tintoretto was not yet thirty when he painted this for the Scuola Grande di San Marco. Among the crowd looking at the slave lying on the ground, you can see the painter himself, young, a short beard, as he appeared in 1548. Not everyone is looking in the same direction, this is the strange thing about it. The hand of a man who is standing diagonally to the right of the painter is pointing forcefully to the left, the light on the nail of his index finger wants us to see that, even though the hand to which the finger belongs is so close to another hand, the hand of a man in blue, who is holding a stick and looking straight down. The crowd is standing still, and yet everything here is movement, and if it is true that Tintoretto wrote "Michelangelo's drawing with the colours of Titian" on the wall of his studio, that can certainly be seen here. He did wonders with white, the gleam of armour, the folds in a sleeve, the windings of a turban, the halo of a man of the air who, as in the Last Judgment, is flying through space, in a wide flowing cloak, everything ensures that you are there as a viewer, that you are looking along with them. And I look once again at the painter, who is standing with his shoulder next to the foot of two classical columns, not far from a man or perhaps a woman with a bulbous pink turban. The story has it that the painting was both admired and criticised and so the offended artist took it back home. Forty years later, he was commissioned by the city to paint *Paradise,* in which there are so many people that the absurd idea of my imaginary piazza is no longer so strange. Tintoretto was old and fragile then, he could no longer find the happiness that should reign in a paradise, the vain Venetians who all wanted to appear in it were perhaps too powerful for him, or was he nostalgic for the time when he could simply stand at the back of a crowd in which he had depicted himself, a young man looking at a miracle among people he had painted?

Slowly I begin to penetrate my new neighbourhood. In the morning I am woken by footsteps passing by in the alley or by the loud ringing of the first human creature I will see that day, a man or woman in a luminous uniform, who wants to have my light-blue rubbish bag. Glass and plastic some days too, they are keen to have it all, and woe betide you if you simply deposit it somewhere by the bridge or in the alleyway. I have asked what I should do if I am not at home one day, and they told me the location of the boat where I must leave it. The nearest café is for students. I like sitting there, if only because I never went to a university and so I view them with a certain anthropological curiosity. March seems to be the time for exams, sometimes I see a young woman there with a kind of floral wreath on her head, surrounded by a circle of peers who are singing to her because she is now a doctor, one of the many graduates who must try to find employment in a country where there is little work. The café is next to the only baker in the area, on Fondamenta dell'Arzere, for the rest of my shopping I need to go further afield. Nothing here seems old, in the evenings the café closes early, sometimes I have breakfast at a table outside, among the students and their somewhat dusty later form, the teachers. When the newspaper is free, I read the *Gazzettino*, not so much because of the ups and downs of the world, which seem distant here, but more for the local news, because for me here that is the real news: legal cases, political squabbling with unknown names, finally a new book, it makes a change from Trump and Merkel. Later in the day it becomes a little busier, from a table outside the café I look at Rio Arzere, calm water. There is a bridge over it to the Quartiere Santa Marta, new construction with no excitement, places for people, a dead zone, which I know only from the vaporetto, passing by from the station and along Canale Scomenzera to Zattere and onwards to the Lido. What you see when you are on board are the big garages (for the carless city) on one side and a vacant undeveloped lot on the other, with rails ending in nothingness, a no-man's-land, which turns into the streets where I am now walking, into yet another Venice, which here seems like a large stage for an unimportant play without a plot and with sets by a not particularly gifted designer. The main actors are not yet there, what I see are bit players like me, a young woman with a child, an old man taking a dog for a walk, a postman, a Dutch writer who is wandering about looking at the signs and notices, while the real author is still sitting at his desk, unable to come up with anything. But fortunately there are other people who can write. Someone has found a black cat and wants to return it to the owner, but has forgotten to include a telephone number, maybe there is some kind of drama there? And Carlotta is looking for "small objects", such as *ninnoli* and *cianfrusaglie*, whatever they might be, to do some arts and crafts. By an empty patch of land, there is a large round sign on a brick wall with the words *Giardino Liberato* written on it by hand, liberated garden, and beneath that *curalo, vivilo, difendilo*, care for it, experience it, defend it, but no-one has listened, as the image is one of immense desolation. How do you show that, desolation? I think of the absent author and, in his stead, I write the directions for his play: "An abandoned patch of grass, stage left a half-perished rubber car tyre, torn in half, the wall of a house, painted yellow, neglected, a couple of white plastic chairs, fallen over or leant against a table, a rusty fence to the right, random rubbish scattered on the ground, paper, a cardboard box. In the distance a government noticeboard, signs made illegible by the rain." All that is missing is the *dramatis personae*, but I can picture them all a little, young women with torn jeans and men, also young but already bald, with jihadi beards.

Sometimes you need to recover from too much beauty by visiting the other Venice. And as if it is meant to be, I read, in an article about Brexit by John Gapper in the *Financial Times*, a quote from the English scientist and novelist C. P. Snow that seems strangely fitting for the desolate image in front of me: "[The Venetians] had become rich, like we did, by accident. They had acquired immense political skill, just as we have. A good many of them were tough-minded, realistic, patriotic men. They knew, just as clearly as we know, that the current of history had begun to flow against them. Many gave their minds to working out ways to keep going. It would have meant breaking the pattern into which they had crystallised. They were fond of the pattern, just as we are fond of ours. They never found the will to break it." And, as if the absent author at his desk has just woken up, I see beyond the houses by the deserted site the enormous white outline of a gigantic cruise ship sliding past, an ill omen. On the deck stand people who will be let loose in Venice for one day and who will not come to visit this neighbourhood.

Teresa's Garden

THERE ARE CHURCHES IN VENICE THAT YOU HAVE SEEN a hundred times and yet have never entered, until the day comes when you suddenly *really* SEE the church you have seen a hundred times and realise that there was no sensible reason why you had never actually noticed that church before, as it is a building of great beauty. So I should phrase the question differently: Why is it that we do not want to see some buildings? My nonsensical answer in this case: too close to the station. The railway station of Venice is modern in an uninteresting way, it is always busy, and busy and modern do not belong right next to a church from the seventeenth century, and so a certain degree of holiness is lacking, stations are commotion, departure, farewell, and yet I have come here to stay. Opposite the station are a number of vaporetti with the corresponding stops, the 5.1 turns the corner to the lagoon just past that church, the 1 quickly heads past and into the Canal Grande, people with rolling suitcases are walking all over the quayside in front of the church, you can hardly take a couple of steps back to look up at the façade, let alone go inside. It is not only the invisible future that can spirit away buildings one day, the past can do it too. In a painting by Canaletto, I see four or so unadorned, rather bare and austere buildings in the place where the station is now, compared to which the Carmelite church must have seemed to its contemporaries in 1680 like a miracle of exuberance.

I remember the moment I first saw the church from across the water. With unexpected astonishment, you start counting the columns on the front from afar, look at the waving figures high up on the triangular pediment, see that two of those figures may well be sitting uncomfortably on the sloping sides of that isosceles triangle, as if they are on a slide, and then notice that there are three others, one of whom is standing all alone up on the tip of that façade, you wonder who the five of them are, then discover all kinds of other figures in the niches between the columns, and then it is done, you were standing halfway along Fondamenta San Simeon Piccolo and because you cannot walk across the water, you now have the choice between two bridges to reach the front of the church, which is practically attached to the station, but of course that is not right, it is the station that has nestled up against the church, with only the narrow Calle Carmelitani between. On my large map of Venice you can clearly see it. It is a map in six colours, the entire cobweb spun over the centuries is on it, the built-up areas in light brown, with the important buildings and churches a little darker, yellow for the piazzas and important *fondamenta*, white for the streets and alleyways where you can find or lose your way, blue for the water of the lagoon and the canals and rios, green for where there are no buildings, and green dots for the *giardini*, the parks. Stazione Santa Lucia lies along Fondamenta Santa Lucia like a modern-day invader, black lines lead the way there, the tracks approaching from the mainland and across the lagoon, all the way to the neatly drawn light-brown platforms where the rolling suitcases disembark. Next to all this is the church I had neglected for so long, Santa Maria di Nazareth and its monastery, the monastery of the Discalced Carmelites, a name that leads you to assume that there are also Calced Carmelites, which is indeed the case. This is the monastery of the Scalzi, as they are known here, the monks without shoes, the Order of the Carmelites. With Romanesque and Gothic, I generally stay on the ground, as human beings should, but with a Baroque church like this, I would like to have wings, simply to zoom through the space and, like some kind of giant humming bird, to hover in front of the main altar and take a closer look at the twisted columns of red French marble, and then slowly to allow my eyes to go upwards, so that the foam of those chillingly white marble Corinthian capitals frothing up onto those columns may have its effect on me from as close up as possible and to pause there and watch the ordered insanity of the Baroque flying up to an extremely exuberant crown and dome. How far all of this is from the simplicity of the Romanesque or the cool austerity of Protestant Dutch churches. Luxury, opulence, splendour, as if this were about a different God, a God who could revel in the way marble and gold had been forced into this geometric swirl, a rampant proliferation that is at the same time order. An Austrian bomb during the Second World War put an end to a fresco that the young Tiepolo had painted in the vaulting, and so I will never see it, and later when, back on my feet as usual, I walk through the church, I am reminded in a different way of absence and mortality, because in one of the side chapels I find the grave of Ludovico Manin, the last doge, who was allowed to hand over Venice to Napoleon, the end of the dream. Because this is some-thing you realise when you are back outside, that you are in the humble, later, flip side of that dream, the seamy side of the fabric that once expressed power in this place. This city is trapped in its own past. Nostalgically or unknow-ingly, you walk around in a preserved archaeology of a lost but still-present empire. I do not know what the founders of the Carmelites, the two mystics Teresa of Ávila and John of the Cross, would have made of all this. They are standing between the twisted columns of the main altar, but not far from them there are also statues of the mythical pre-Christian Sibyls, which I know from antiquity, enigmatic female prophets like the Sibyl of Delphi, and that takes you into yet a different order of time. I remember the Latin hymn "*Dies illa, dies irae*", which I sang or heard in my youth and in which the words "*teste David cum Sibylla*" appeared. But Teresa of Ávila knew that hymn too, so what is here is both an anachronism and a wondrous simultaneity, a church like a kaleidoscopic fairy tale, in which the two reclining figures of Cain and Abel have to share the triangle of the pediment with Adam and Eve, but also with Christ giving his blessing. What would Teresa have thought? Would she have felt at home amidst all this excess of form and meaning? The question is a legitimate one. She came from the most desolate land imaginable, the parched plain of the Spanish *meseta*, the monastic order she founded had to do with the earlier anchorites of Mount Carmel in the Holy Land, long before her sixteenth century. Men who lived alone, for whom prayer and meditation was their entire life, perhaps even in their own time they were aliens. It is the twelfth century, then in 1226 the Order of the Carmelites officially becomes a part of the Church, they worship Mary and are inspired by the prophet Elijah, all kinds of things come together here, even the mysterious words "discalced" and "calced" assume a meaning, and it is not about bare feet, but rather with or without sandals. When the monks, after the Crusades, had been driven out of what was then still called the Holy Land and had to abandon their destroyed monasteries in Asia, and the Pope decided they could no longer live in Europe as hermits but instead as a mendicant order, Teresa of Ávila founded a small monastery. A woman founding a monastery for men, you can only really believe it after you look at the painting Velázquez made of Teresa of Ávila at the moment of her inspiration. Like Carpaccio's Augustine, she is holding a quill pen in her raised hand, the light on her face comes from the dove in the gold-coloured cloud that sends out a ray of light as thin and sharp as the pen she holds in her hand. In the present day, it is hard to enter into another person's mystical rapture, this is a very Spanish image of a very Spanish woman, but her single-mindedness is visible in that painting, and it can still be read in what she wrote, which is far-reaching, a passionate quest for God and, in my opinion, it does not matter how a later age tries to reflect upon an almost-erotic mystical ecstasy, it was real for the person involved, just as it was for the poet and mystic Hadewijch. Not long ago I watched an old Spanish film about Teresa, and even though mysticism is hard to film, I have not forgotten those slow images, covered wagons travelling through the landscape I know so well, the sound of horses' hoofs, the infinite emptiness as the small caravan moves across the plain, a landscape that forces you to think about your place in the world during those long hours of travel. Carried in a litter, the silent nun in her black and white habit, her face twisted in pain because of some unspecified illness, and then that same white face in the immobility of the apparent death that would follow the journey and last an implausible length of time, a living dead nun. Later episodes in the film show a woman who had been to a place where no-one else could follow her, and who had returned. The objective of the film is that we should understand what kind of era this daughter of a family of minor landed gentry, descended from converted Jews, lived in, how poor the Spain of the conquistadors was and how turbulent and uncertain the age. The gold that the colonists had brought back to Spain had resulted in a huge devaluation of money, the country was at war with northern Protestants, the nobility was impoverished, agriculture was neglected and yielding nothing, in the film the noble houses are dark spaces through which people wander with candles, it is a world of extreme characters in which Teresa writes her books and, on her way to her sudden great inspiration, draws up her rule. The new order had to be a contemplative one, a life devoted to the quest for God as the only reality, the way there described in clearly defined stages, such as "Interior Castle", words and concepts from a different era that still buzz around on the Internet for those who wish to look for them. The church and the monastery of the Scalzi in Venice are a distant echo of this, a thought rescued from time, which has travelled such a very long way from that harsh Spanish landscape to take root in the spiritual landscape of the Counterrevolution and the later excesses of the Italian Baroque. As well as the Teresa of ecstatic visions, there was also a very logical and practical woman, someone who understood that she had to take what had once been a congregation of seekers of God living in isolation on Mount Carmel and reshape it for the new age. The arid Spanish land from which she came, the passionate prose she wrote, the Baroque that transformed her asceticism into an architectural counter-dream, puzzles that the later visitor must try to solve.

How can a book become a garden? The day I visited the church of the Scalzi, I picked up a leaflet off a table, which mentioned a garden.

Gardens in Venice are rare and seldom open to the public. I gathered that the monastery had a garden that could be visited by appointment. When I called a few days later, I detected a certain hesitation on the other end of the line, but after another few days permission arrived, along with an appointment. We reported to a small office next to the church, on the station side, and were then introduced to two ladies. I could, of course, call them women, because these ladies were that too, but the one who looked like the older of the two, the one who spoke first, had that aura, recognisable always and everywhere, of good intentions and the upper classes, perhaps what Nijhoff in a poem called "a scent of higher honey". The other lady was more earthly, maybe she came from one of the islands in the lagoon – who knows?

The pair of them formed a perfect contrast that morning. What was certain in any case was that they were in a state of great uncertainty, but in order to explain that I have to return for a moment to Teresa and the book she wrote later in her life about her mystical search for God, *The Interior Castle*, a path for the soul in seven stages, in which the soul must overcome doubt, temptation and all kinds of other obstacles before the goal is reached. The point was that these thoughts had later found an earthly form in the shape of a garden that alluded to the order's connection to those original twelfth-century anchorites, and at the same time to the stages the soul had to pass through to reach God. In *The Interior Castle*, Teresa writes about "seven mansions". The terminology of mystics is not simple, and when I read that kind of thing I always feel as if I am heading off into the mountains without skis, but it came down to the fact that this garden contained medieval, numerological, medicinal and botanical secrets to guide the soul, all clearly reflected in the layout of the garden, and the only problem was that the garden was now in great disarray, and so the ladies were visibly confused, and I could not pretend not to have noticed. I am not relating this story to make fun of them, far from it, I understood their misfortune and perhaps even shame, they had not been in the garden for a long time, and the monks (there were only four of them) had told them they could no longer take proper care of the garden, or they had been let down, the monk who had always looked after the garden had departed for another monastery, the explanation was along those lines, which sounded like a warning or rather a perfect illustration of what can happen to the soul on its way to higher things. It is not for me to bring up the Devil, but there *was* something devilish about it, a meticulously crafted design thrown into chaos by human incapacity. The book that came with the tour showed a plan of the garden as it was intended, with clearly delineated plant beds, a "numerological layout", accompanied by a question apparently from Einstein: "How can you put Beethoven's Ninth in a Cartesian diagram? There are realities that cannot be quantified. The universe is not captured by my numbers; it is pervaded by mystery. He who has no sense of mystery is half-dead."

Armed with that serious thought, we set off, a contemplative little group, in search of a lost meaning. The garden is elongated, running parallel to the railway lines; they must be next to us, but we cannot see them because a wall is in the way. We stroll with the ladies along the paths and the beds of plants named according to numerical symbolism. I cannot help taking occasional peeks at the book and I spot something about twenty-one being the number of all the different plants that are or should be in the garden, but then I get lost in the notion of twenty-one as divisible by seven, but also seven times three, and seven and three as sacred numbers and I wonder what Teresa and Einstein would have made of

that. Medicinal herbs, the "orchard of lost flavours", I look and I listen to the ladies, but now that we are accustomed to the idea of imperfection, a strange calm comes over me, from behind all those walls I hear trains and vaporetti, the noise of the world, but here we have the ladies' singsong and the slow beat of our footsteps in this *hortus conclusus.* I wonder what it would be like if everything were intact and in full bloom, a holy meditation spot bursting with meaning in the middle of this city of gondolas and lions. We have found our way to the end of the garden, a few chilly-looking trees stand there, they are all different and that too has a meaning, I feel that we should console the two ladies, so when we are at the exit I buy a bottle of Acqua di Melissa, which the monks used to make here, but it now comes from the monastery in Verona. Even so, I have the feeling that I have been permitted to see an unknown Venice here. A gardener is digging somewhere, so perhaps there is still hope. We thank the ladies, say that we have learned a lot, which is true. For a moment, in the midst of Venice, we have been in a mystical garden and a deserted corner of Mount Carmel, and a March wind has risen, chasing us out of paradise, but at least there is no angel with a flaming sword.

Giacomo and Teresa

A story of two worlds

IN THE INFINITE RANGE OF POSSIBILITIES FOR HUMAN behaviour, it is hard to find a greater difference between two people than between the ascetic but passionate mystic Teresa and the equally passionate Rococo personality of Casanova, who pursued his own goals with the same diligence and consistency, a very personal method of study and an indefinable form of discipline that, to his contemporaries, must have looked like debauchery. You could also attempt a similar comparison between Hildegard von Bingen and the Marquis de Sade, but that would get you nowhere, no, with Teresa and Casanova you can at least imagine an encounter between the two, a conversation in a monastery garden or on the stylised balcony of a Venetian palazzo, an exchange of thoughts with no physical implications, but with intellectual ones, a *discours de la méthode* or a dialogue Diderot might have devised. Venice is a part of Casanova's life, along with the opera, carriages, masks, Carnevale, travelling and the rustling silk of women's clothes, particularly as they are being removed, quickly or perhaps slowly, to lie in soothing silence beside the bed where the naked lover waits. He too was a writer who, like Teresa, wrote a book about his so very different life, which was not accompanied by a symbolic garden, but was about forms of love, and which, like Teresa's *Interior Castle*, is still read today. A film was made about him too, one that I saw years ago, and I now know that the filmmaker, whom I admired immensely, had fallen prey to a complete misunderstanding about the individual who was the subject of his film. Fellini, because that was the filmmaker in question, saw Casanova as a sex-obsessed robot, an automaton, and there are, if I remember correctly, moments in the film when he even made Donald Sutherland move like an automaton, a stiff, mechanical doll with white make-up, wound up with a key, somewhat sinister in my memory. Strangely enough, that is more or less all I recall, that and those silk, lace and satin sounds of clothes that could be taken off. Now that I am once again living in a narrow alleyway, there is one aspect of life here that I cannot ignore. The window opposite, which is usually shuttered, and the sudden light that shines through its cracks. There is nothing palatial about this alleyway, but the sounds, and above all the visual possibilities offered by such an alleyway, can be exciting enough for someone with voyeuristic or other erotic inclinations. In this city, there are also palazzi that have an alleyway at the back, there are scaffolds, quays, balconies, corners, a possible geometry of the hidden, the sudden opening to a canal, the darkness of a cellar. The eye is a camera that can go anywhere. A window that is ajar, a half-finished sentence that you hear, some whispering in the semi-darkness, someone walking by in a mask, a certain hurried way of walking, a door revealing the shadow of two people just before it shuts, everything from the arsenal of the silent film, as it is never disturbed by the sounds of cars. Gestures of silhouettes on a bridge, the swish of a voluminous cloak being swung around a woman's back, the splashing of oars, at night this city still keeps her secrets, she keeps them but does not hide them, shows them in the form of a puzzle or an enigma. Chandeliers seen through high windows, the people behind those windows like dancers without music, a shuttered water taxi gliding by apparently with no-one at the wheel, a seagull flying into the air, a gondola at night with two people and a silent gondolier, the footsteps of the passer-by who is you in the territory of the dead hours, when in the distance you can feel the watery presence of the lagoon as an endless black plain encircling everything and seeming to rock the city to sleep with all its stories. These are the hours when the imagination works, when hidden images want to become words. The buoys in the water gently move, as if they are the commas and full stops of a story that you should tell, a story of your previous self in this city, someone who has disappeared, been forgotten, dissolved into the transience of which there is so much more here than in all the other cities you know, and at the same time a strange light-heartedness because the world here is simply as it is, a masquerade without a mask, a face for a single existence.

It must have been on a night like this that Casanova, incarcerated by the state inquisitors in the Piombi, Venice's prison of horrors, tried to escape. There was no film yet, so why do I see it as one? Then, in 1756, it was a November night, slowly moving towards All Saints' and All Souls' Day. Now it is March, the light is just as sparse, the chill coming from the lagoon must have been the same. The camera is focused on the lead sheets on the roof of the Piombi (*piombo* means lead), the prison from which no-one has yet escaped. No-one except for the imaginary viewer sees one of those sheets, literally as heavy as lead and riveted to the marble gutter, slowly rising. The camera zooms in, briefly we see a pair of eyes through the narrow crack in the light of that winter evening, before the tombstone slowly and silently sinks back down into place. Giacomo Casanova has seen what we already know: that it is a clear night over Venice. The waxing moon, which will come into its first quarter the following day, would have made a shadow dance out of the escape on the high roof. The would-be fugitive pictures it: elongated shadows on the paving stones of Piazza San Marco in the otherwise unilluminated city. The moon will not go down until eleven, and then there are another eight and a half hours until the sun comes up. The man under the lead roof, about whom Philippe Sollers will write that he spent five seasons in hell, knows he must wait the eternity of another three hours. He has led the reckless life of an adventurer, a lover and a gambler, someone who even now is putting everything at stake. It is this, or humiliation, or death. But he is a daredevil with self-control, this master of suspended ejaculation. An adventurer who can calculate, a chess player, a strategist. A man who has led a life focused on getting in must also be able to get out. Just before the fatal hour, he writes in the cell of Count Asquini, as he says "without a light": "It is the duty of our Lords, the State Inquisitors, to use every means in their power to keep a guilty man in prison, but the prisoner, if he is not on parole, should do everything he can to escape. Their right is based on justice, his on nature. They did not ask his consent to imprison him, he need not ask theirs to set himself free."

I can only see the film I am seeing in my imagination because the escapee, towards the end of his life, wrote an account of his escape so vivid that it takes your breath away even today. His endless scraping with a "pike" into the wood under the lead plates, the rope of "a hundred fathoms" that he made himself out of sheets and blankets cut to pieces and tied together with "weavers' knots", the silk cloak and handkerchiefs and stockings that he also had to sacrifice, you can picture it, just as you can also see the disguised priest, who is escaping along with him, clutching Casanova's belt with the four fingers (four! after all those years he can still remember) of his right hand as Casanova works his way up the roof.

Anyone who wants to know what it was like will have to go there one night, when the moon has gone down and the music on Piazza San Marco has died away, and stand alone on that square and try to imagine it without the light of the lampposts. What you will then see and hear is darkness and silence, and in that darkness and silence you will have to imagine two men straddling the highest point of the roof, two hundred steps away from the voluptuous and bulbous oriental domes of San Marco. Of course, it should not happen that at that moment the monk's hat falls from the roof and slowly, as if ceremoniously doffed several times, swoops down into the water far below, and all those subsequent Hitchcockian moments of terror and doubt should equally be forbidden, but the rope, the hat and the terror are all elements of the story that a few weeks later will be making the rounds of all the European courts, along with the impenetrable barred window, the despair, and then the sudden crashing ring of twelve from the Campanile, so close, the moment when the brilliant freethinker up there on the roof realises that it is now the feast of All Saints, and that among all those saints there must be one who is willing to protect him.

I first encountered – although did not really read – Casanova the writer in German long ago, published in Berlin and Vienna, *vollständig übertragen* by Heinrich Conrad. Purchased somewhere at a book market, six volumes, yellowing paper, broken spines, Gothic letters, my German not yet good enough. But why did I buy it? It must have been in my puberty, the name Casanova had a mysterious appeal, merely by owning those six brown books I would, according to Schopenhauer's adage, also own their contents, and so share in an unapproachable world that was represented by an ungainly female figure (*Die Tänzerin Camargo*) in the second part: the laced-in waist, the high bosom, the porcelain ankles under the wide skirts where the secrets must be located that had been so extensively studied and mapped by the author. As I write that sentence I hear how ridiculous it sounds in an era of nudist beaches and bikinis, of male chauvinist pigs and political correctness. Casanova would not have stood a ghost of a chance in our age of extreme visibility, which seemingly cannot wait for a new fundamentalism to flourish, or for everyone to die of televisual fatigue.

Years after not really reading those six German volumes and before I bought the magnificent English edition in Venice, I had occasion to interview Federico Fellini about *his* Casanova, and stung by the perversion of chronology, which means sometimes you know more later than you did before, I would now like to conduct that interview again, because back then I had no response for him. What has happened in the meantime? Voltaire, Diderot, Talleyrand, and reading the book by the man in question, that is what happened. The book by Philippe Sollers, *Casanova l'admirable*, had led me to rediscover the old libertine, along with new editions of his memoirs in French and Dutch, the great spiritual storm of the enlightened eighteenth century, when they thought the world was being recreated in chiaroscuro, shallow yet profound, a theatre through which those figures, more than life-sized, had danced, writing, scheming, thinking in beds, salons and at desks, with, in the background, the encyclopaedia and the guillotine. So what would I say to Fellini now? That, since reading the remarkable book by the Hungarian Miklós Szentkuthy (*Marginalia on Casanova, St Orpheus Breviary* Vol. 1), I think Giacomo Casanova loved women more than all the male feminists of the twenty-first century combined? The conversation with Fellini must remain as it is, especially because it is a portrait of the maestro I still so much admire. But now I would like to join Sollers in saying that this twentieth-first century will come to nothing unless we can once again find the spirit of the eighteenth century.

On a gloomy day at the end of the previous millennium, I visited the Piombi for the first time. Last to wear out are stones and iron bars, I wrote at the time. What you can still see there is the essential idea of prison: infinitely thick doors, gigantic locks, the mere sight of which is barbaric, words of desperation scratched into the wall, barred windows whose interwoven mesh of rounded wrought iron depicts the fatal impossibility of escape. More than two hundred and fifty years ago, a theatrical adventurer, a delightful swindler, a quick-tempered poseur, a lover who is passed from one woman to another on the basis of his service record (according to Szentkuthy), a failed all-rounder and a brilliant writer, who, like Stendhal, knew his worth, flew out through these impenetrable bars because much later, old and lonely at the end of his life, he still had a book to write, somewhere in a Bohemian castle, the story of an unconventional fantasist who dreamed up his own reality in such a way that we still want to read it.

It could well be that I am alone in being surprised at the different possibilities of the human species, with Italian men voluntarily hiding themselves away in a monastery as followers of a Spanish nun, while barely one hundred years later, in the same city, another specimen of the human race tried his utmost to escape from a cell. It takes all sorts, as they say in English. A city is only a city when over the course of time so many contradictions have accumulated there that it defies explanation.

The woman has come to collect the rubbish, we have wished each other a good day, and it looks as if this wish will come true. A light glow of sun is clinging to the dead church on the other side of Rio di Santa Maria Maggiore, which owes its name to the invalidated church, I have placed a wobbly plastic chair that came with the house out among the weeds in the pitiful garden with the intention of continuing to read a story by Borges that I began yesterday evening. It is quiet on the water. On the quay opposite, a man is taking the tarpaulin off his small boat, but a cargo boat with all kinds of vegetables goes past, so his boat begins to rock and he tries to keep his balance, a small ballet. The neighbours' washing is hanging over the drooping bush between two windows, I try to guess the composition of the family by looking at the various items of clothing. Strangers' laundry always has a hint of forbidden intimacy, and there is plenty of that in Venice. In some narrow alleyways, the washing hangs across the street, and you can sometimes dream up whole novels based on it, as those clothes, which can tell you quite a lot, will soon be put onto human bodies that you may try to imagine. I had found the story by Borges in an old book I had brought with me from the Netherlands and had chosen that specific story because the title intrigued me. I had already read it once before, but could not remember exactly what it was about. The title, "The Garden of Forking Paths", made me think of a labyrinth, not least because I knew Borges was obsessed by labyrinths. A few years ago now, I was allowed to stay a month in Venice at the Fondazione Cini on the island of San Giorgio Maggiore, where they have designed not only a magnificent garden and a glorious library, but also a labyrinth of plants that is dedicated to Borges.

Simone took a photograph of that labyrinth of plants at the time, probably from a higher window of the former Benedictine monastery, and when I look at that photograph, I always have a dizzy sensation, not exactly pleasant, maybe it is because in that threatening story by Borges the one who is telling it knows that you can get lost not only in space, but also in time, and that at the end of the story he will die. The box plants come to about halfway up your body, and all those carefully trimmed hedges enclose the claustrophobic, gravel-strewn path along which you have to find your way, even though it is constructed in such a manner that you think you will never get out of it again. What you do not see in that photograph is an entrance and so (I do not know if "so" is the right word here) there is no exit either. They must exist though, because to get lost you first have to venture within, after which the moment inevitably comes when you most definitely want to get out again. Maybe that is why I like the Dutch word for labyrinth so much: *doolhof*, "wander-garden". *Dool* comes from *dolen*, "to roam, wander, go astray", and it is a word that is almost extinct, existing only in old texts and in that one word, while a *hof* is a garden or

a courtyard. The English call a *doolhof* a maze, which in turn has a Dutch connection, because when I look up *maas* (plural *mazen*) in the Van Dale dictionary, it says "each of the openings formed by the crisscrossing lines of a mesh, expr. to crawl through the *mazen* of the net, fig. to narrowly escape". I am not sure whether it is because of the thought of that photograph or the story by Borges or the narrow alleyway where I live or the eternal cliché of Venice as a labyrinth, but when the protagonist of the story has met his fatal end and I want to go out for a coffee somewhere, I find myself standing in the doorway of my house on Calle de Madonna, not knowing which way I will go. I am standing directly opposite the house in front of me, the one I can touch from my window upstairs, so I cannot go straight on, now I myself am at a point where the paths fork. Whether I want it or not, this must be the entrance to a maze. But where is the exit? And does Venice have an exit? As always, I have a map of Venice with me and I decide to allow myself to be caught, without thinking about it, in the *mazen* of the mesh that is this city, in search of an exit. In Borges' story "Ibn Hakkan al-Bokhari – Dead in his Labyrinth", one protagonist says to the other that it is wise to go left at every fork in a maze. So, in order to get a better overview, I walk left. That is one decision made. At the first bridge I come to, still close to my house, I sit down for a moment on Fondamenta delle Procuratie. As if someone has issued a prohibition, I make a deal with myself that I will not take the boat even once, and that I shall come up with an imaginary exit, and see to it that I get there. And then I decide that this is all nonsense, that I will simply walk on without using a map, which means venturing out into the city with my eyes closed for once, with the intention of ending up on the other side of the city.

Game without a Map

I DO NOT WISH TO OBLIGE MY READERS TO DO ANYTHING, but I would suggest you look at a map. What is on the other side from where you are, and how can you get there without taking a vaporetto even once? Then, in the Venetian wander-garden, you can start at any random point and try, without the map, to end up on the opposite side, wherever that might be, we all have to determine that for ourselves. Mine is the end of Castello, where San Pietro, the former cathedral of Venice, is located. Why? That enormous church is on a small island, which is therefore called Isola di San Pietro, and I feel that it is where the city ends, because you are alone there, looking out across the lagoon without immediately seeing the other side. That is where I want to go, using my instincts alone, without a map and consulting no-one. There are street signs all over the city, after all, I am not here for the first time, and I know where I want to go. And of course I did find my way there. In the story by Borges, Ibn Hakkan al-Bokhari, who had designed the labyrinth in order to escape his fate, dies surrounded by those infinite walls he had built himself, and I did not intend to do the same. However, I can advise anyone who has the time to try this at least once. Choose a random point, head there without a map, never taking a vaporetto but only bridges, it is worth the effort. No matter where you are, everywhere is Venice, and where there are fewer people you find more surprises, if only because you can literally see more. I no longer remember exactly how I did it. It was reasonable weather, some wind or other was blowing from the north, changing the colour of the water, I was a passer-by among strangers who all had a goal, and I heard my footsteps among those of all the others, and then suddenly it was quiet again and I heard only my own steps in a narrow alleyway where no-one else wanted to walk. What strikes you then is how many signs people have left behind, faded emblems, depictions of animals and professions, things that are trying to say something I can no longer understand. This city is a storehouse for the past, everyone has left something behind, has carved something into a wall, did not wish simply to disappear. I had walked past the front of the station, then past the Scalzi, past the church and the garden I now knew, then turned left off the Canal Grande into a big shopping street, and across a square with a church, but where it seemed to make sense to go straight on, I found myself near the Ghetto, sat down on a bench in a piazza and noticed how deliciously sweet it smelled there because there was a bakery nearby, so I paused to eat something with an incomprehensible name, thought about how close to the east this city has always been, and then walked on, sometimes everything seemed very familiar, like Fondamenta della Misericordia, which told me I was near Santa Madonna dell' Orto, a bridge, a street, an alleyway, a detour, the wall of a palazzo, turn around, a coat of arms, a year, another wall, a dead end at the water, and suddenly Fondamenta Nove with the vaporetto stops (forbidden in this game) to the islands and the cemetery, then the lions of the Ospedale with their wise old faces, then keeping right, getting lost three times and finally there was Schiavoni, with its memories of Yugoslavia and Dalmatia. After that it was no longer such a challenge, as I had also lived in these neighbourhoods for a while, which had left me with an affection for Via Giuseppe Garibaldi, not only because of the statue of the hero, which looks as if he might burst into song at any moment, but mostly because of the garden behind him and the street at his feet, as that street is wide and so completely normal, shops, cafés, newspaper kiosks, a street that could be almost anywhere and where for a minute you are freed from everything, because children are playing there, old ladies in wheelchairs are being pushed hither and thither, men of my age who already know it all are discussing the problems of the world over glasses of wine the shade of Homer's wine-dark sea. Further on, the street narrows to two quays on either

side of the Rio di Sant' Anna, the houses there are a little sadder, I see how the water has left its traces on the bricks, as water too is a writer that leaves nothing untouched, biting into the Istrian stone, just as it penetrates the chestnut wood of the mooring posts, active every second of the night and day, licking and eating at the stones and bricks, leaving a warning of how high it can rise, it knows that one day it will overcome this city, it nibbles, licks, sucks and munches and never stops, just as the wind, coming from every direction, perhaps with some hail or rain thrown in or the scorching bite of the desert dust, has had free rein here for centuries. Brick is vulnerable, all the elements are an enemy, when the plaster spread over it turns from white to grey and then black and finally flakes off, the brick shamelessly shows its red interior, which slowly discolours to a deathly yellowish shade of decay and defeat, that too is a story told by the bricks of Venice, which also know the even harsher law of ultimate fate: that not even the hardest and most gleaming marble is immortal. Every boat passing by, no matter how small, helps to write the story, the pedestrian that is me wishes to cross Canale San Pietro, can already see the leaning tower that stands close to the church but does not belong to it, from here I know every metre, I have arrived on the other side of my labyrinth, I am approaching the way out, I know this wall, where a plant I cannot name grows at eye level, I remember him or her from last year, this is my favourite puzzle: how can a plant, green and strong, emerge from a closed wall, what infinite willpower does it require, no soil, just bricks and mortar, the wind blowing a tiny seed into a minute opening, rain, damp air from the lagoon, and an unquenchable will to survive against all the odds. I would like to know what this plant is called in my own language, if only because the names of the humble can be so beautiful. I would like to call her *steengroeier*, stone-grower, and the man I could have asked about it, who wrote one of my favourite books about Venice, is dead. He was called Predrag Matvejević and he wrote a book in Croatian about this city that, for once, was not about palazzi and churches but about the different forms of mooring posts, the names of the objects that have disappeared, the tools that the shipbuilders used throughout all those centuries, about the different kinds of bread that once were eaten here, which could be traced back to the cosmopolitan worlds the Venetian ships brought back from overseas, but also about what I call the humble, about the plants no-one ever notices because they grow at the level of our feet, living out their almost invisible existence on the edges of canals, between the steps of churches, on walls and under bridges. I almost said nameless existence, but that is not true. In his book, which in German is called *Das andere Venedig*, his plants do have names, there they are called *Seebeifuß, Leinkraut, Schöllkraut, Wasserklee, Kornelkirsche. Beifuß* is, in my language, *bijvoet* or *alsem, Leinkraut* is *vlaskruid*, my dictionary remains silent about *Schöllkraut*, *Wasserklee* is *waterdrieblad*, and *Kornelkirsche* is *kornoelje*. Sea wormwood, toadflax, greater celandine, bogbean, Cornelian cherry. I have got that far, but now I need to recognise them. With his book in my hand, I went to look under the bridges where he had found some of his plants, but unless you are on a boat it is hard to search under bridges, although that is where he had seen the *kornoelje* that is known as *muraiuola* in Venetian, "because it clings to walls". So is that my plant? Armed with the photograph, I will, before I write the last words of this book, have found it. Meanwhile I remain grateful to Matvejević, because he has given me a tour of a different Venice, a place where you have to look in all directions to see what you would never have otherwise seen, such as the half-naked woman who, in her left hand, is holding up the dress she has apparently just taken off. She is high up on a crimson wall in plaster relief, someone wanted to tell us something and we no longer know what it was, her face under a sort of turban looks terrified, as if she needs help, and part of her right arm has disappeared. Someone should write her novel, the story of a half-naked woman high up on a wall in a different century and someone – who could it have been? – wanted us to see her, but why?

If Venice is an island made up of islands, then San Pietro is an island outside that island. It is beyond everything, just about hanging on by two bridges. If that crooked campanile and that big church, where once the patriarch of Venice lived, were not there, who would still go to the island? A few streets, a small park in front of the church, where old ladies take their dogs for a walk, it is enough for me. The campanile stands there, misunderstood, tall, at the top an invisible relief that can be meant only for angels or birds, but in order to reach the tower you have to go down a couple of small streets, and you are startled when someone comes around the corner. After the bridge I turned left and am standing by the water. It is low here, brownish, strangely shaped aquatic plants drift to and fro, the underwater plants are the other inhabitants of this city. Immediately after the water, the street here is called Quintavalle, you see, in the wall where you turn the corner, a damaged relief. Lorenzetti's wonderful old guide, in which every stone in Venice is described, knows its name: he calls it *un tabernacolo marmoreo*, a marble tabernacle. If I did not know this was Mary, I would see a woman on a throne with a child on her lap who is handing over some keys to an old man. The man is wearing a three-tiered crown, a tiara, and if you know what a tiara is in this case, you also know that you are dealing with a pope, and as he is holding a large key, he must be Peter, the first Pope of Rome. The enigma of images, if they meant only what you literally see, they could give you strange ideas. For a moment I imagine I am a Chinese tourist from Xiangzhou, who has wandered away from my tour group. What would I see? A child with just one leg, on the lap of a young woman whose skirt has become a rock, a stone bird frozen in position over their heads. A story, no doubt, but what does it mean? I always stop in front of it, this time someone has placed a pot with purplish flowers there, the leaves look like sage. Nothing has changed about the image, but that of course is not true, two furious artists, wind and rain, have been working for centuries on this relief, and when they finish their work, it will disappear. These were once, says Lorenzetti, the *estremi limiti della città*, this is where the people of the first confederation of the islands in the lagoon came, when the city was not yet built. When you know that, it makes you walk a little differently. Later I see Olivolo on a street sign, as olives used to flourish here, and it is called Castello because there was once a fort here that the first Venetians built to defend themselves against invaders.

There was apparently a church in this place even before the year 1000, with a bishop who was subordinate to the patriarch of Grado. Later in history this would result in great and irreconcilable rivalry, which Pope Nicholas V eventually resolved in 1451 by making the bishop of this church patriarch of Venice. The small park in front of the cathedral is empty, the wind that comes across Canale di San Pietro through the thin trees and blows away the dust in front of the church knows all about history. Until 1807, this was permitted to be the most important church in the city, and after that it was San Marco.

In the distance I see the high, forbidding walls of the Arsenale. What once must have been the patriarch's palazzo looks sad, neglected, the walls damaged, paint peeling, there are supposedly Byzantine elements that can be seen inside still, but the building is closed. In a deserted courtyard I shelter from a rain shower, and then I go into the church beneath the angry adolescent face of a fully grown putto with thick lips, suspended between festoons above the entrance beneath the classical, always-soothing forms of a follower of Palladio. Other than the woman inside a glass box who is there to sell tickets, there is no-one to be seen. The building is huge, what will become of these mammoth structures? I once stood in Segesta in Sicily, in the vast empty temple of Poseidon/Neptune – who should have told the faithful back then what would become of their temple after their gods had disappeared?

I suppress these blasphemous thoughts, because for now the original inhabitant is fortunately still in residence, and only if he were to disappear would the question really become pressing. Or macabre, like the corpse of Lenin in Moscow, put on display with make-up on its face. But here, too, the dead are not far away, when I turn right in the enormous space, the first thing I see is a sarcophagus at an unimaginable height on the wall. I do not understand why the Venetians sometimes accommodate their noble dead so high above their heads, perhaps it has something to do with an eternal fear of high water. High and dry, but that means no-one can ever get to them, and you cannot see the sculpted figures beneath the coffin he does not lie inside but rather upon, unless you use powerful binoculars. And because my child's soul always takes everything literally, I wonder how it feels to lie there for centuries so motionlessly and to listen to the footsteps of living people you never knew. Filippo Correr was his name, one of the noble names of the city where nobility had the power, *procuratore*, an important function in this sea republic, the brother of Pope Gregory XII. When I walk on, I come to a marble chair festooned with Arabic, verses from the Koran. Venetians stopped at nothing, lions from Syria, columns from Byzantium, a quadriga from Constantinople, everything was taken home, just like this Arabic marble throne, upon which Saint Peter apparently sat, the world was their property. A helpful sign translates for me what the Arabic calligraphy on the backrest means, lines from Surah III, verse 194: "Our Lord, and grant us what You promised us through Your messengers and do not disgrace us on the Day of Resurrection", and beneath it Surah XXIII, verse 118: "My Lord, forgive and have mercy, and You are the best of the merciful."

The woman in her ticket booth is so far away, and there is still no-one else around, so I dare for a moment to touch the chair and, with my fingers, I follow the arabesques of the text, the geometric lines of the Star of David, wondering as always whether it could perhaps be true after all that Peter sat against this ornate backrest from Antioch, a fisherman from Israel who proved that history is a riddle without intention, but certainly with consequences, the masked fate that is nothing without people. If the world is everything, then history is everything that constantly happens, and there is a marble chair with Arabic letters in an Italian church, almost fallen into disuse, on an island on the edge of a lagoon in southern Europe. The fact that the backrest is actually a tombstone that was used to turn it into a throne has long since ceased to matter, no more than it matters that it is impossible for someone from the first century to sit on a chair from the thirteenth century. Legends are the marrow of history, and everything they tell is true.

I have only to walk further into the church to see that it is true. In the giant wall painting by Pietro Ricchi in the chapel to the right of the main altar, I see the three kings. I do not know whether they really existed, but we have known for centuries what they were called and which gifts they brought to that stable in Bethlehem, and here you can no longer doubt, as Ricchi has painted them as if he were there, horses, riders, trees, slaves, trumpets, female bodies, all in swirling motion and among them the three powerful men in their voluminous robes, two kneeling with their gifts, the third standing with the light on his white turban, his gleaming cloak open wide, the golden gift in his left hand, the grey horse not far behind, prancing and neighing, anyone who looks at it is there, Hollywood cannot compete, the noise must be deafening, I am standing here in a deathly silent church that is far too big, but when I turn to the other side, it becomes even worse, as opposite the kings Pietro Liberi has painted a plague of serpents to terrify the viewer. Later I had to consult the Book of Numbers in the Bible to know what I had seen, the people of Israel on their way through the desert with Moses, angry, unhappy, dissatisfied, grumbling against God and against Moses: "Why have you brought us out of Egypt to die in the desert? Because there is no bread here, and no water, and our soul is disgusted by this miserable food." That culinary reproach must have been the last straw, as punishment followed immediately, "for the Lord sent venomous snakes among them, who bit the people, and many people of Israel died". Anyone who complains that there are too many tourists in Venice can take a rest in San Pietro di Castello, here the crowds are only painted ones, the walls tell ancient stories. History has no aim, only consequences, people have intentions, and what happens then is painted here on these walls.

Filled with everything I have seen, I wander for a while in the empty streets behind the church, and because this city is a book that turns its own pages, I read, in letters carved into a weathered wooden board, that someone wants me to think about the golden medal of Giovanni Sanguineti, once the lieutenant of the 71st Regiment Fanteria, who fell gloriously for the fatherland in Coatit, Eritrea, on January 14, 1895. With reverence and love, it says underneath, and again I wonder if history has a goal or an aim. What we call history is unimaginable without people, and people always have intentions, but are people the makers or merely the material of history? And again I come to a sign, I shall call it that, yet more people wanting us to express gratitude, this time to Arciprete Giovanni Cotin. They were the inhabitants of this neighbourhood behind the church, which is called Quintavalle. Beneath a statue of Mary, in honour of the priest, they have made a small slot in a sort of money box, which was built into the wall in 1915–18. Another puzzle I will not solve today, and when I try to insert a modern coin on the off chance, it does not work. An *arciprete* is an archpriest, but when later I ask the Internet what exactly that is, I find something about a priest from a parish in Eindhoven, which fell under the Patriarchate of Constantinople, and so I am back in Venice. I walk around this quiet extremity of Venice for a while, this must be the way out of my maze, Calle di Mezzo, Calle Lunga Quintavalle, Fondamenta Olivolo, then the San Pietro stop, and the lagoon, which lies before me, wide and smooth and a little misty.

Here, too, I am the only one. The water is very still, black

with an undercurrent of grey. For a moment I imagine I could walk on it, but then a lonely boat approaches from Rio di Quintavalle with an old man in it, drawing a wrinkled furrow in the metal that was just now so immobile. On board he has two large fishing rods and a net, and I wish I could go with him. It is as if I have been far, far away from the city.

Among Lions

ASTROLOGICALLY SPEAKING, I AM A LEO, A LION. SO MY number is 1 and my metal is pure gold, and my profession should be king or banker, which is all fine by me, but in general I have never paid too much attention. The horoscopes in newspapers and women's magazines are never accurate, they never dare to predict anything terrible. No-one ever dies in them and there are never any serious warnings, so that you could decide, for example, not to take the plane you booked for next Tuesday after all. The only tribute I pay to my star sign is that, when in zoos, I invariably visit the lion enclosure to gaze at the pride with sensual delight, if only to see how majestic the head of the family looks. Not because I think I resemble him, because that would require a real mane that would make your head twice the size. Not only that but you would also have to behave in a way that befitted that head, holding it directly above your front paws and staring straight ahead, without taking the slightest notice of the fuss and nonsense around you. Wherever he lies down, he is always the centre of attention, and he knows it. It does not surprise me at all that the lion is the totem animal of Venice. The only other male they can stand to have around is a learned saint, such as Jerome in the desert, as painted by Carpaccio and Hieronymus Bosch, or Mark, who wrote the gospel and, eight hundred years after his death, was abducted by the Venetians and taken, lion and all, from Alexandria to the lagoon. On my wanderings through the city I encounter the lion everywhere, in wood, in bronze, in marble, in plaster, there is nowhere that he is not. Sometimes he has an open book with him, *Pax tibi, Marce, evangelista meus*, peace be unto you, Mark, my evangelist, it says on the two open stone pages. Usually he also has a magnificent pair of wings. That is how Carpaccio painted him, evidently quite furious, with long wings extending far behind him. In the background to his right there are some ships, in the distance the Doge's Palace. The painter has also given him a halo, he has his right paw on the open gospel of Mark, everything is exactly right, this lion is the city. I have tried to imagine it, a flying lion. It must make quite a noise. He is older than our common calendar, Jesus was yet to be born and Mark still had to write his gospel. He must have landed like that one night on the pillar, a fabulous animal from the Byzantine East keeping watch up there for almost nine hundred years now. In all those years he has descended from his high pedestal only once, and that was when Napoleon took him home. We know how things turned out for Napoleon, maybe the exiled emperor on St Helena sometimes still dreamed of that lion who had already seen so many empires come and go. From the piazza you can only truly see his vast proportions with a pair of binoculars. Over all the years I have put together a collection of photographs of lions, and the differences are breathtaking. If you look closely, the one on the Piazzetta has an angry old man's face above a high Babylonian collar, and I know furious, calculating, senile, political, toothless, hysterical and amorous lions. The one in the Museo Storico Navale is made of gold-painted wood, not only does he have a sword in his right paw but he is also wearing a crown. Sometimes the lions look grief-stricken, at other times they look as if they have been waiting for someone for centuries. The one at the monument to Vittorio Emanuele II on Schiavoni is of a heroic and Wagnerian bronze, the one at San Giorgio Maggiore can barely hold his book and is sad, the wooden ceiling lion in the Scuola Grande di San Marco is caught in his own golden wings, you wish you could see them one day all together in an immense field of lions or in a fleet of gondolas on the Canal Grande, perhaps a show of gratitude for their years of service. My favourites are on the wall of the Ospedale near Giovanni e Paolo and the large sorrowful kings guarding the Arsenale, once the nuclear power station of this city. This is where the ships were built that conquered a colonial empire, they still stand powerfully before the doors

through which you are not allowed to enter, and I imagine they know that the great empire has had its day. Such a thing might happen, that a marble statue changes imperceptibly over the course of centuries and, as power dwindles, perhaps a gradual melancholy appears on those faces, once so fearsome. On the day Venice disappears beneath the water, all the lions of the city will ascend like a deadly squadron, fly once more around the Campanile with the sound of a hundred bombers, and disappear across the lagoon like a mighty solar eclipse, leaving the sinking city behind.

Death and Venice

WATER HAS NO PAST, SAID THE JEWISH POET IN THIS city full of water. It was the city he loved, where he now lies buried at his request. He lies close to the anti-Semite who was also a poet, who also lived here until he was arrested and banished, and who returned here to die. They lie here together, their posthumous conversation is silence, but they are here because of everything they once said, a Russian and an American, Joseph Brodsky and Ezra Pound. I have tried to write Paradise, says Pound in his last Canto, but in the Second World War, midway through the grandiose arc of his Cantos, he raced unbridled towards his later shame. Brodsky hears, in one of his poems, a gondola banging against its moorings, he thinks about the drowning city, where the dry light of reason flows into a moistened eye, thinks about the winged lion of the city, a lion that can read and write. Somewhere else he sees three elderly American ladies in a hotel lobby, or, in a sentence I can no longer find, he writes about murky, money-coloured water.

PAX
TIBI

VAN=
LISTA
C. LA

In her book *Sidewalks*, Valeria Luiselli searched for the grave of one and found an old woman with a bag full of things by the grave of the other. That woman knows who Pound was, she calls her dead man "*il bello*". She does not know Brodsky, but they start talking. Luiselli writes about that conversation in her book and quotes Brodsky. "If there is an infinite aspect to space," he says, "it is not its expansion but its reduction. If only because the reduction of space, oddly enough, is always more coherent. It's better structured and has more names: a cell, a closet, a grave." Pound knew all about cells. After the American occupying forces arrested him for treason, he was first imprisoned in a cage and later in a mental asylum in the United States. A cage is the ultimate reduced space. Brodsky lived for a long time in a universe of hotel rooms, and a hotel room is also a reduced space, as I know from experience, so if there is an infinite aspect to space, these two dead poets know all about reduction. Luiselli says, "To locate the grave, the definitive inscription we're looking for, it's necessary to examine the veining of the marble closely." She looked for the grave of one and that led her to the other, then she speculates that Brodsky would have preferred to be buried elsewhere, which I do not believe, but as she says herself, "If will and life are two things impossible to separate, so are death and chance", and she continues, "Brodsky occupied many other temporal spaces [...] But perhaps a person only has two real residences: the childhood home and the grave. All the other places we inhabit are a mere grey spectrum of that first dwelling, a blurred succession of walls that finally resolve themselves into the crypt or the urn – the tiniest of the infinite divisions of space into which a human body can fit." As for myself, I do not remember the house of my earliest childhood, and I do not yet know my final place of residence, I am still in the phase of the vague succession of hotel rooms and walls, and there are plenty of those in Venice.

If you walk along the Zattere to the tip of the Dogana, you pass the famous guesthouse La Calcina – the house where Ruskin once lived, which has since become an expensive hotel. In the past I used to stay there occasionally, but this time I behave like a tourist, sitting in a womb-like armchair and ordering a whisky that is brought to me by someone from distant British colonial regions. Not far from La Calcina is a brick wall with a simple plaque stating that Brodsky often stayed in the house behind it, the home of a noble Venetian friend. Through a gate you can catch a glimpse of the house and the garden, but that is all. On the cover of his *Collected Poems in English*, which I have with me, he sits relaxed on a bench on a quayside, with his eternal cigarette, legs crossed, left hand in the pocket of his jeans, someone who did not necessarily want to be photographed. With a slightly ironic smile, he looks into the camera. He had a bad heart, was not actually allowed to smoke or drink, but disregarded that advice. It must be autumn or winter, judging by the peeling walls of the house behind him, it may also be Venice, through one of the windows a chaos of furniture and antique frames for paintings, possibly a second-hand bookshop. In the book I seek out the poems that have to do with Venice. What strikes the reader of *Watermark* is the lightning-fast eye through which everything he sees and thinks is processed with an undertone of melancholy; in the poetry, it is the rapid succession of kaleidoscopic images, with a combination of that quickness of seeing and thinking and a form of sadness, especially in the longer poems.

He sees a rundown rusty Romanian tanker sailing by, in the long seconds that this perhaps takes he has already seen through the lives of the semi-naked men at the ship's rail, masturbators and womanisers, with no money to afford female company after so long at sea, and he also sees what those men on board must see, Venice like a postcard pinned up to the sunset, the vision of an enchanted city after a lengthy journey from the desert ports where all that oil comes from, conjuring it up in nine times two lines, just one single page, and yet a complete picture of yearning for the impossible.

The Jewish Cemetery

INFECTED BY SO MANY THOUGHTS ABOUT URNS, GRAVES and death, I decide to visit the Jewish cemetery on the Lido, where Brodsky is *not* buried. A few years ago, a friend from Amsterdam asked if I knew whether it was ever open. She had twice stood in vain at the gate, and now wanted to return to Venice because she was determined to see that cemetery. I promised to find out, took the vaporetto to the Lido, where everything is so different from on the other side of the water, walked along a few silent streets, saw a narrow, closed gate with a burning menorah above it in a blue mosaic, and in Greek letters below an Alpha and an Omega, but in reverse order. As a traveller you are familiar with locked doors, if you wait long enough or walk on to the next door, then, as long as it is not Sabbath – and today it is not – something will open up.

There was a larger entrance nearby, I saw no-one and walked through, and five minutes later an amiable guard with a kippah in his hand caught up with me, a little out of breath.

A skullcap is such a tiny item of clothing, a small piece of fabric, but still it makes something happen, you turn, just a little, into someone else, slowing your footsteps and becoming part of your surroundings in a way that cannot entirely be fathomed. Maybe this is what they mean by mimicry. I know the Jewish cemeteries of Prague and Berlin, I know that graves in such cemeteries are not supposed to be emptied, that they can sink deeper and deeper into the ground, that everything that the inexorable passing of time can inflict on different sorts of stones can be seen there, that the enamel of photographs can be so affected by time that the dead man in the picture would never recognise this stranger as himself. I also know that gravestones, if they are old enough, end up standing crooked in the ground, as if they themselves were old people. Words, in Hebrew, German or Italian, wear out, names break into pieces, families are torn apart. There is a German word, *Ruinenwert*, literally "ruin value", and it is present in abundance here, the graves have made a pact with nature that they will reinforce each other, a blackened gravestone with letters that are now illegible in tall waving grass, a fallen column beneath a palm, an obelisk in the shadow of a cypress, the two elevated sarcophagi of a married couple on a high pedestal, his name has been erased by the wind or by time, but hers is still there in the sunlight, Lavinia, and on the pedestal below, still just about possible to spell out, letter by letter, Levi or Levy. I am struck by the crooked angles of most of the graves, the eroded iron enclosures, the rusting fences around horizontal broken slabs, and another truncated column beside a tall tombstone adorned with flowers, *A Mose Romano, nato a Padova 1810* with, far below it, a sentence in Hebrew, which I cannot read. Is this a place of chaos? No, it is the order of decay, but the silence around me makes it a curious sensation, like finding yourself at a party from infinitely long ago, where everyone has suddenly frozen. The tall gravestones lean towards one another, as if bowing and curtseying, Elia Vivante, Fanny Sforni Vivante, Ignazio Sternberg. Samuele della Vida, who lived more than ninety years ago *senza vacillare un instante*, "without faltering for a moment", bows to his neighbour, the giant tree beside them is preparing to fall upon them both with all its leaves, everything is possible here now, the illegible names, the veiled Hebrew, the dancing shadows on the fallen stones, all a mixture of misery and another sentiment that is much harder to interpret, perhaps an almost inexplicable joy because the world is as it is. Suddenly I wonder if Brodsky ever walked around here. What would he have thought beside the grave of Esther Finzi Coen? Anyone who has ever read Giorgio Bassani's *Il giardino dei Finzi-Contini*, or seen Vittorio De Sica's film about Jewish life in this part of Italy and how the war and hatred put an end to it, knows the forms of nostalgia for the past that has gone for good, which make you stop at this grave because something impossible and incomprehensible is expressed on this stone too. I cannot read the years; the veining in the stone, as Luiselli puts it, offers only puzzles. What do those two hands mean, pointing upwards on that ancient oval stone above the Finzi of her name? I can decipher *continuare*, to continue, but to where? Above those two hands, with their fingers slightly spread, I see a crown with three pearls. Did those hands want to have this crown, to put it on? Or is there a hidden meaning that someone could explain to me? I stand there a while, looking at the broken branches, the withered laurel leaves in her little enclave, and leave this Esther alone among all those others she knew or did not know. On the way out I deposit my kippah in a basket among the other kippahs. I see another large outstretched hand with a hole in it where I can leave my obol, and I remember my mother, who said to me so many times: son, you have to learn to be careful with money, you have a hole in your hand. She was not buried, my mother, but blew away on the wind. For a moment I think she is beckoning me with that hand with the hole in, and perhaps it is true.

Posthumous Mountaineering

A CITY WHERE SO MUCH HAS HAPPENED, WHERE SO many different living people have dwelled, has also produced very different types of not-living people. Among the dead of Venice, the doges are the mountain climbers. They did not want to go into the ground they loved so much; as in their lives, they wanted to go higher. You can see the results in the big churches, the Frari, Santi Giovanni e Paolo, San Marco. They do not have peaceful graves where you might bring a flower or kneel for a moment or leave a note, no, you cannot reach them, they and their retinue have already climbed high up the walls, halfway to heaven, if you want to see them you have to stare up and take care not to get dizzy. There were one hundred and twenty doges, fewer than there were popes (that number has now reached 266) but more than most kings and emperors.

The first doge was Paoluccio Anafesto, a ghost from the marshes, leader of the island people who populated the lagoon on their flight from the hordes. They did not really belong anywhere, these nomadic seafarers, not even in Lombardy, so nearby. The real counting does not begin until later, in the days when the Venetians also began to escape the influence of Constantinople. In 697, the boat people scattered throughout the lagoon chose their first doge, and in those early, hard-to-interpret years you also hear for the first time the names that will keep coming for centuries, Dandolo, Memmo, Loredan, Foscari, Morosini, Tiepolo, Zen, but what really happened takes place in a twilight where legends can thrive and families that later become important can invent their origins, following the maxim of the older, the better, a thought that would persist for more than a thousand years. Choosing a doge was an extremely complicated process, established once and for all in 1268. Between one thousand and two thousand patricians, all men, of course, gathered in the Doge's Palace and received at random, from a boy with an urn containing as many balls as there were voters, a ball that they had not chosen. Among all those balls there were thirty made of gold. If you received a golden ball, all your family members had to leave the room. Now they had no chance of getting a golden ball, tough luck, but any appearance of nepotism had to be avoided. New ballot. The number of chosen ones is reduced to nine, who put forward forty names. Each of those forty needs to receive votes from at least seven of the nine electors, but we are not there yet – there is another ballot, golden balls are drawn again and the forty become twelve, who have to put forward twenty-five others, who are reduced again to nine. I have no idea what kind of mind you must have to come up with such a thing, but if you have ever seen an illustration of a cross-section of the human brain, you are getting close to the answer: those nine choose forty-five, only eleven of whom shall be chosen by golden balls to be the electors of the electors of the doge. These eleven now select the forty-one chosen ones, whose names have not featured in any one of all those previous lotteries, and who will ultimately choose the doge in a conclave, and he must have a majority of twenty-five of the forty-one votes. Perhaps now you see what I meant about climbing mountains. The two doges whose graves I am visiting were men who went through all of this. Their place of rest is high above the congregation on the walls of one of the most beautiful churches in Venice, the Basilica di Santa Maria Gloriosa dei Frari. Their names are Francesco Foscari and Nicolò Tron, they were doges numbers 65 and 68. If this Francesco wanted us still to be thinking about him centuries later, then he succeeded. He lies up there, high and dry among four virtues, depicted as women, of course, on his bed of state, his head tilted a little to the left. Two martial-looking warriors hold open the golden curtains around his bed. His coat of arms, embedded in two brightly shining suns and with the doge's cap on top, accompanies him to eternity, so they know who they are dealing with up there too. It is a tall and slender grave, Christ holds the soul of the departed in his hands, but he is standing so far away that you can barely see it.

Francesco Foscari ruled for thirty-four years. He was an enemy of that other powerful family, the Loredans, who tried to have him killed in 1430. And even before he became doge in 1423, he had enemies. His predecessor, Tommaso Mocenigo, warned of his tempestuous character in his will. He waged war against the Visconti, won a considerable amount of land in the Peace of Ferrara, four of his children died of the plague, but he had enough of them left. Twenty years later his last surviving son was sentenced to eternal exile on Crete for a murder he had not committed, and died before he was pardoned – troubled times. In 1457, Francesco died, and it is a miracle that he is still wearing his cap on his stone deathbed, because in real life it was taken from him a week before his death by the Council of Ten, who had forced him to abdicate. I cannot make out his doge's ring up there on his tomb, his right hand is lying in the stillness of death and I cannot see the left one. The ring had been destroyed on the orders of the Council of Ten. Nearby, and even higher than that of the humiliated Foscari, are the five storeys of the grave of Nicolò Tron. He ruled only briefly, in years of threat. During the reign of his predecessor, the Ottomans under Mehmet the Second had already started to advance, his son had died at the Siege of Negroponte, Venice had lost two of its most important colonies, he sent the fleet under Pietro Mocenigo to pillage the Greek islands and destroy Smyrna. Calmly, he stands in an alcove on what I shall call the first floor of his monument, two floors higher he is depicted again, now lying, unlike his predecessor Foscari, with his head slightly to the right. In total I count twenty-four figures, big and small, human and divine, accompanying him in his eternal stasis. The Caritas beside him at the bottom, sculpted by Antonio Rizzo, is as pretty as a picture, in the most literal sense. An almost-oriental pensive face, a twisted braid down her neck. The history of art consists of folds and pleats, someone once said, and I cannot help but think of that when I try to follow the lines and creases created by the narrow band under her breasts, as delicate and free as the folds of the robe that her left hand is lifting. It is hard to believe it is not fabric, but marble. All the years of the Middle Ages are forgotten, Rizzo has boldly reconquered an antiquity, these sculptures are accompanied by a nostalgia for Ovid's *Metamorphoses*, the power and the glory of an imperial Rome.

How many doges' graves can you visit? Even in death they seem to be competing with one another. Doge 81, Francesco Venier, ruled for only two years, and according to Amable de Fournoux he was not well loved by the Venetians, but in his high grave in San Salvatore he lies sleeping beautifully in his ermine shoulder cape, and Doge Leonardo Loredan, number 75, is in Santi Giovanni e Paolo, arms outstretched among allegorical depictions of the League of Cambrai and the military might of Venice. The problem with allegorical depictions is that sometimes they reveal little of the past reality: a young woman with something like Greek *cothurni*, small high breasts and a somewhat blind gaze staring into an unknown distance is intended to embody the coalition that had been agreed between the king of France, the Pope in Rome and the emperor of Austria in order to put a stop once and for all to the superpower of Venice, and the sturdy young man with the shield and baton on the other side of the doge is supposed to embody the power of the Venetian army, which lost some of its possessions on the Italian mainland in 1509 at the Battle of Agnadello. If they had left it at that, then Loredan might not have been able to rest here quite so peacefully, but the friends of the League became one another's enemies, changing fronts, betrayal on all sides, until Venice won back almost everything at the battle of Marignano.

I sit there, calm and quiet, the clashing of arms has become inaudible, the blood invisible, most of the dead no longer have names, but this one does, and otherwise there is only history, which looks like a number of classical statues in graceful postures, draped around a man who appears much younger than the eighty-four years that Leonardo lived. As I come out of the church, I wonder how many eyes you would need in order to think you have achieved at least some kind of understanding of this city. This city never ends. In the Jesuit church I see doge 88, Pasquale Cicogna, sleeping blissfully on his side, his left hand under his head, but I also know that he is the one who surrendered Giordano Bruno to Rome, where he was ultimately burned alive, and that is unforgivable, even if Cicogna's name is still on the Rialto Bridge.

Perhaps it is not appropriate, but I also have a favourite doge, Enrico Dandolo, and he is not buried in Venice, but where he died, in Constantinople. I must have seen the grave a few years ago in the Hagia Sophia in Istanbul. Not a grand monument, a simple stone, and that suits him. I have to go back in time for him, to a pageant play, to the crusades, to the major international politics of those days, to Byzantium and the thirteenth century. This Dandolo was over eighty and almost blind when he was chosen, a powerful spider in the web of what was then the known world. Always hard to imagine, no newspapers, no television, no Internet, communication travelled on foot, with voices in secret rooms, with the scratching of quills on parchment. This is obvious, and yet it makes you stop to think: horses, ships, messengers, whispering, secrets, discussions, spies, rumours, the pitfalls of different languages, the king of Armenia, the king of Hungary, war with Pisa, insurrection in Dalmatia, and then the fourth crusade, a fleet sailing out, shouting, cheering, flags, opera, scenes from a movie, and then only the silence of the lagoon after the fleet has sailed, the great piazza empty, the footsteps of the crowd until the last few stragglers return to their houses and palaces after the final ship has set sail, the breathless wait for the first reports. Doges, doges and more doges, when you read Norwich's history of Venice, it seems as if you have gone astray in several historical novels at once. Perhaps it is because of the Byzantine aspect, an eastern world in which events and legends intertwine, but the endless succession of struggle, punishment and reward in the history of the city that was an empire is almost too much for a book, this calls for big screens, operas, choirs. Dandolo was number 41, I go back in time for him, first humiliation, then order once again, treading water, the empty pages of the history book Hegel talks about. Only then does his moment come.

You might wonder if it is wise to have Enrico Dandolo as a favourite doge, but the image of an octogenarian blind man, embarking on the Fourth Crusade, not reaching the Holy Land but sailing only as far as Byzantium, where he has a number of things to do and dies in 1205 after having refused the Byzantine crown but still dismantling the splendid quadriga and sending it back to his hometown, is an irresistible one. The four horses that Napoleon would steal from Venice six centuries later were just a part of the spoils of war. The whole Byzantine Empire is divided among the crusaders, and Dandolo and his successors become masters of "a quarter and a half" of the Roman Empire. According to Norwich, "no-one knows for certain" that Dandolo was really blind or really eighty-four when he was elected, but in *La Venise des Doges*, Amable de Fournoux sticks both to blindness and to that age, and that is how I see him sailing away from Venice on his ship, no doubt satisfied with the great poker game he has just won against the allied fleet on the Lido. How do you write history? Both Norwich and De Fournoux read Geoffroy de Villehardouin on this Fourth Crusade, later generations are at the mercy of chroniclers who have heard the story from other chroniclers, nothing is invented, all being well, but anyone who wants to retell everything is drawn into the web of stories and is wise to keep to the facts, to what we are certain happened. If we think that a complicated German government coalition, a Brexit, a Korean dictator with deadly weapons and an unpredictable president of America are problems, then perhaps it is useful to imagine Enrico Dandolo who, after Venice had agreed in 1201 to equip a fleet for the Fourth Crusade, a crusade in which not only Venetians but also Flemings, Germans and Frenchmen would take part, succeeded in bringing together 4,500 knights, 9,000 squires, 20,000 foot soldiers and enough food for nine months, as if an enormous child would be born after those nine months. The cost: 84,000 silver marks.

*

Contracts were signed. Everything was agreed, everything up to and including the day, June 24, St John's Day. Not everyone knew exactly where the voyage would take them, duplicity was the order of the day, and Dandolo's secret intention was to go to Constantinople and not to Jerusalem, and when this leaked out, perhaps not entirely by accident, fewer than a third of the armies turned up. Venice had kept its promises, the fleet was there, but who would go on board now? And who would pay the 84,000 marks? Would the whole crusade have to be called off? Dandolo played a magnificent game of poker. The troops who were already there were not permitted to enter Venice, the narrow Lido was the place they were all gathered, and nothing was happening now except for endless waiting. The doge knew that the troops who were there had counted on significant spoils of war, Constantinople had the reputation of being an Eldorado, and to simply go back home now was not an option.

Poker is poker: not one ship was allowed to leave the harbour until the payment had been made. And again the moment dawns of a Spielberg Hollywood scene, a Mass in the basilica where the old doge with a cross on his *corno* addresses the troops and says that he – in the words of the chronicle – is prepared to sail out with them and the pilgrims and to live or, if necessary, to die. The following scene sees the fleet sailing away, the doge's ship leading the way, vermilion, the sound of trumpets, cymbals, singing, wind in the sails. It will not be a glorious journey, a week later they have already recaptured a Croatian port, the Franks and the Venetians start fighting over the division of the spoils, and this is just the beginning, a year later Constantinople will be destroyed, humiliated, plundered, set on fire, an unimaginable bloodbath, sacrilege or, as the chronicler Nicetas Choniates describes it in words that are crying out to be painted by Hieronymus Bosch, horses and donkeys in the church, gold and jewels stripped from the throne, golden chalices stolen, a whore on the patriarch's throne, and all of this in what is now the city of Erdoğan, because there too history has never rested. And Dandolo? He receives the 50,000 silver marks he is owed, becomes involved in the selection of the new emperor, and is able to reap further profits, dominion over the Mediterranean from the lagoon to the Black Sea, and dies in 1205 in the imperial palace, far from his beloved Venice. His grave is on a gallery in the Hagia Sophia, once a cathedral, then a mosque, now a museum. We do not know what he would have thought of that, perhaps it is true what Norwich writes at the end of his chapter, that it was because of the crusade led by this Dandolo, which had nothing to do with the cross, that the Eastern Roman Empire and the entire legacy of Greek and Roman culture that was gathered in Constantinople would decline and fall to the Ottoman Empire two centuries later. San Marco, Santa Sophia, from one church to another, but all that remains of Sophia is the name, once a holy mosque with the grave of a doge from Venice.

Maybe it is because I am from Amsterdam, but with all the stories about Venice, I cannot help thinking about the similarities between the two cities. Like Venice, Amsterdam was small, compact, but also for a time the capital of an empire, with settlements on distant shores. Trade was the driving force. In Amsterdam, too, those who could not set off into the world themselves could buy shares that would allow them to participate in all the adventures. Amsterdam was no more feudal than Venice, there is a reason why the Heren, the gentlemen, come before the Keizers and the Prinsen, the emperors and the princes, in the Amsterdam hierarchy of canals, the merchant class of citizens was the real nobility, the Dutch East India Company played the same role as the Great Council in Venice. Venice and Amsterdam were both cities of painters, and perhaps it is only the irony of history that both cities are now overrun by tourists who come to look at the relics of that distant past. Like Venice, Amsterdam is a city of water, and like Venice Amsterdam was in a sense a republic, as it was a part of the Republic of the Seven United Netherlands. In old prints, there are ships at anchor in both cities, and a little nostalgia has always lingered for the good old days and lost empires. This is perhaps where the comparison stops, but it might explain why the city on the Adriatic keeps pulling me back.

Stories in Pictures II

Giorgione in the Accademia

ONE OF THE MOST ENIGMATIC PAINTINGS BY THE ALREADY enigmatic Giorgione is called *The Tempest*, and it hangs in the Accademia in a not particularly conspicuous place. I was not looking for it, but for something else. One of those rare moments, you have walked past something and yet in fact you have already stopped. In the complex maze between eyes and brain, a lever has been pulled, I had to stop, I had to know what was happening to me. Now that I have looked at that painting countless times, I still wonder what it was, what *exactly*. There was a meaning that had to do with me, and I did not know what that meaning was. It was painted, and at least for the time being I was still real. Did I want to be in the painting myself? But who would paint me? The wall of time between us is invisible, and yet I cannot go through it or over it. What is the secret? Not the unearthly light, not the flash of lightning in the billowing clouds, not the glint in the leaves of the thin trees back by the city wall. The woman, naked but for a white shoulder cape, is holding a small child to her breast. The child is drinking but she is not looking at it. She is looking at me, and that means at every me who is looking at her at any given moment. This must also apply to the painter, although he could not have been standing there in that landscape. He saw her in his imagination. It is not certain whether the young man with his long staff and his very festive shorts is looking at her. I cannot tell in any case. His chin is slightly raised, he seems to be smiling, he belongs to the picture without belonging to the woman. But he is there, the painter took time for him. And yet if I were in his place, she would not be looking at me as she is now. Does she know that I am looking too? If she did not, she would surely be looking differently, wouldn't she? This is taking place between us, that must be it.

To the left of the young man is something that could be a chimney if there were a house attached, but there is only a small wall, with upon it two columns? pipes? tubes? gleaming in the sunlight, a foreign object that increases the enigma of the whole. But why did I stop? It can only be because of her gaze, an expression somewhere between suspicion and curiosity, as she recognises me, or the invisible other person who is looking, across time, as if she knows something about me, or him. She sits, her bent, naked left leg at a strange angle beside her in the grass, as if she would like to stand up, to flee. The fine leaves of a small bush are drawn almost like a tattoo on her naked skin and like a decoration on the folds

of the white cloth that lies behind her. A bridge, city walls in an ominous light, dark crowns of trees, everything gloomy, and then the colour of her skin, the child lost to the world at her full breast, her white shoulder cape, the young man's white shirt, his indefinable gaze, her suspicion, the puzzle of what she is thinking, and, irrationally, my deep desire to be admitted to that painting, to walk past her, to roam through the city that is lying there as light and radiant as a vision, and eventually, hurried and agitated, to return from that city from the other side, to her, to be with her, to turn into paint and to be invisible at the same time, a painted man beside her on the grass, part of her secret, the impossible, because as I stand in front of that painting, unable to enter, I know that I am hidden somewhere behind those walls or those bushes, that I am waiting and remain waiting until finally I know what she wants. Now it is just about her and me, everyone else has disappeared.

Canaletto

On the cover of the second volume of a large German edition of the magnificent Venice book that has been so useful to me while writing,[2] there is a section of a famous painting by Canaletto that hangs not in Venice but in Rome. It is called *The Rialto Bridge from the South*, but as this is a fragment, the

2 Giandomenico Romanelli, *Venedig, Kunst und Architectur* (Könemann, 1997)

bridge itself cannot be seen, and because it is a photographic reproduction and also because of the gloss of the paper, the painting has assumed an exceptionally dream-like quality. Small arcs have been drawn in the many-coloured water to represent waves, the gondoliers near and far stand in the typical poses of someone who has to propel a boat using a long pole, poses that have not changed over the course of time. Because they are painted small in the painting, which I have never seen in reality, they have no expressions, which only increases the sense of alienation, perhaps they are ghosts, on the right-hand side of the picture, transparent golden rays of light descend vertically, it must be late in the evening, perhaps even night. Unlike the other gondolas, the one in the foreground does not have a *ferro* at the front, that sculpture like a bird's beak, perhaps so as not to distract from the central figure, who because of his pose dominates the whole picture. He is standing upright, is wearing a voluminous, ochre-coloured cloak, at his neck a white jabot, he emanates power, if this were the beginning of a film, you would know he would become the protagonist. The ochre of his cloak is reflected in the water. His wig makes me think he is actually Casanova, on his way to the casino or one of his adventures. He stands motionless, his eyes are dark patches in the painting, but he is looking at us. Far beneath him sits what appears to be a child, and that child seems to be rowing, but further to the right, with his back towards us, the real gondolier stands. There are people sitting in the second gondola, under the canopy known in those days as a *felze*, but these are used less frequently nowadays; what we can see of them is the form and the colour of a face half turned towards us but clearly in conversation with someone else, who cannot be seen. Who were they? Why do I think they were lovers who wanted to hide? And why do I want to know? How is it that the picture is so suggestive that you immediately want to know who all these long-vanished people were, what they were saying, and this thought alone makes them a symbol of all the conversations that have never stopped in this city, through Canaletto's art you hear their voices without understanding them, hoarse, softly whispered words, just as you

also hear the sound of the oars, of the water against the low underside of the gondolas. Further away, yet more gondolas are moving, black, sailing bats, nearly all the gondoliers are standing on the starboard side, only the gondolier in the rays of light, close to the ochre man, has opted for port. He has no passengers, his weight at the back and the six-toothed bird's mouth at the front keep the flat vessel in balance. The classic poses of all those gondoliers together turn them into a ballet that has stood still for just a moment, perhaps that is why we always want to return to this city, this timeless repetition of gestures has made Venice a part of an eternity that is visible in this painting, a continuous time in which clocks have no authority, and to which, for as long as you keep looking, you may belong.

Tintoretto

I once wrote in another book about the Annunciation, one of the strangest events in history, and how painters have dealt with it, not for theological reasons, but because for painters that event may be a most miraculous one, but also an incontrovertible theological truth and reality, one that they wanted to portray. They must have imagined it as if they were there, which is why the people in those paintings always wear contemporary clothing. A woman who lives with an older man and is not pregnant sits in her room. That room has been given various forms by different artists, but it nearly always looks like a room from the painter's own time. It is no different here in Tintoretto. Joseph was, as we know, a carpenter, but he is left out of it, as we also know. Literally in this case, he is standing outside, by what was perhaps a shed in the garden. In the distance we see a hill, and the man standing outside, near the house, is working among all kinds of planks, rough pieces of wood that can probably still be used, he does not look up, he sees and hears nothing. The Holy Ghost is doing the job that matters. The house is shabby, as you can see by the plaster that has fallen from the masonry,

by the messy pile of bricks still lying at the foot of what was once a column, by the small chair with its seat of woven reeds, frayed on the underside, unfit for sitting on: poverty. The large, meticulously made bed with the deep-red open canopy, which would look more at home in a palace, as would the high, ornate ceiling, is in strange contrast. I shall ignore the flock of plump and naked putti flying through the air beneath that ceiling, although they could give many a cannibal strange ideas. They accompany the events below with the sound of their flight, a *molto agitato* buzzing. The special element here is, as always, the protagonist, Mary herself. What do you think when you are quietly reading – the open book is still in your lap – and a young man with wings comes flying horizontally at top speed into your silent room? How is he going to brake? They are sturdy wings, what would, on an arm, be an elbow is catching the full light, we do not know exactly where that light is coming from, we can tell that there was a strong wind from the wild folds in the winged man's white robes. It is not clear whether the Holy Ghost in his form of a transparent yet golden dove was visible to Mary, a ray of light touches her head and the halo around it. She is startled – you can see that. Her left foot is pointing straight back, she appears to be trying to protect herself with her right hand, her left arm, outstretched in fear, reaches out, fingers spread, to beneath a spinning wheel, how do you react when a flying man comes to tell you that you will be the mother of God? Disbelief, fear, everything can be read in that face, which now looks small in comparison to the powerful body, dressed in heavy cloth, this message has yet to sink in. She still had the face of a girl, she did not yet know what we know, we know the paintings that have been made of her life, the stable in Bethlehem, the three kings, the flight into Egypt and the long, long way to her place at the foot of the cross of the son who is yet to be born, the miraculous, million-fold multiplication of paint.

Unfinished Farewell

TWO WORDS DOMINATED MY LAST DAY IN VENICE: *buran* and *pilone*. The second was a consequence of the first. A *buran* is a terrible storm from Siberia, which has no business being in Venice, and certainly not on my last day, particularly not when it comes racing across the lagoon, killer blades drawn and knocks down a *pilone*, a mast on the Bridge of Freedom, breaking Venice's only land connection with the rest of the world. It takes a moment to grasp what has happened.

You have not really watched the weather forecast on television. There are elections, and because this time no-one knows how they will turn out, you spend all evening gaping at the clothed robot that Berlusconi has become, trying to understand the young ultra-right-wing Giorgia Meloni, who, according to my Italian friends, cannot speak a word of normal Italian, listening to the politically cloaked xenophobia from the other right-wing candidate, Salvini from the Lega Nord, meanwhile forgetting that the real danger today comes not from people, but does in fact come from the east, and that it has plans all of its own. The apartment that a Dutch friend found for us this time was in a sort of elongated courtyard in a side street off Calle Lunga de San Barnaba, where the wind was not permitted to enter. It was quiet there, a couple of windows had a view of two canals, when the wind or one of the few boats that came by stirred the water, all manner of moving paintings were created in the greyish green, and I could watch it for hours. Long before modern painters, wind and water distorted and stretched things and colours, making rectangles ripple and gleam in a way that a window or a wall can never in fact move. Maybe it was because the carnival was over and the polar wind had chased the multitudes out of the city, maybe it was simply because my stars were favourable, but we were enjoying our time there. In the small apartment, we could hear the bells of the Carmini, which every hour played some hymn or other to Mary from my long-distant childhood, sometimes a boat came by, carrying the voices of people, a cormorant had chosen a spot outside our window to dry its wings, the house was conveniently located between the vaporetti of San Basilio and Ca' Rezzonico, there was a fish stall on Campo Santa Margherita, and close to San Barnaba a vegetable boat, there were a couple of very nice bars, I no longer felt as if I had to do anything and I drifted along on the rhythm of the days. It was as if the city, after all those years, had settled inside me, no longer wanted anything from me. The neighbourhood was calm, the worst of the turbulence was over. The palazzi on the canals were still displaying their power; after dark, people walked along the narrow street like ghostly figures, passers-by as I myself had become. Never have I looked at water as much as in this city. When you are sitting on a vaporetto, you have the water almost at eye level beside you, it constantly changes colour and form, the epitome of the liquid city, if you are here long enough the shape of the city as it appears on the map becomes a part of your body, a constant opposition of moving water and immobile stone, the irrevocability of walls, the inexorable end of a *calle* that finishes in a canal, so that you have no choice but to turn around, I have never experienced it in such a way as this last time, which is of course not a last time, because that is something you would never want to admit to yourself. When I close my eyes I see the shape of the city, after all these years there are memories attached to all the *sestieri*, this city will never become mine and yet it will never let go of me either. Friends had taken us to the car park, the familiar helpless struggle with suitcases across bridges of wood and stone, the whining of the suitcase wheels, which there was talk of banning in Venice, but they will be part of this century until something else is invented, the harsh irregular rhythm of the paving with its large slabs hacked out of distant mountains, the car on the top floor of the car park like a contaminated exile: farewell, for the umpteenth time. Or so we thought. The *buran* had other plans.

We had not even left the car park, and the traffic on Piazzale Roma stood stock-still.

What was striking was that no horns were sounding, a sign that Fate had struck and had been recognised as such, you do not honk your horn at Fate. You stay in your car, getting chilly. The Piazzale is the only place in Venice where you can drive, or as in this case sit in your stationary car, it is also the starting point and terminus of the large yellow buses that serve the Veneto, but they could not leave either, and neither could the blue bus to the airport. It felt a bit like Berlin back in the days of the Wall when you wanted to get out on a Sunday. From the city, you can reach the railway station in Venice by way of two high bridges, but to exit the city entirely you can only leave via the Bridge of Freedom, and that was, as it now turned out, blocked. The enormous concrete column lay right across the bridge, and it was dangerous because of the power lines it had brought down with it in its fall, it was going to take at least an hour, the fire brigade had to come and it was not straightforward. An hour became two hours, then three, then four, and at five we gave up. *Crolla pilone, Venezia nel caos*, wrote the *Gazzettino* the next day. The friends who had brought us to the car park had stayed with us, now we could go back with them to their high-up apartment opposite our old one, the consolation of pasta, a wine from Sicily and a grappa to forget the cold. As we had thought we were leaving properly this time, we had left the keys in the apartment as we were supposed to, and the owner braved the icy night, crossing the Dnieper and the tundra to open up the apartment using an X-ray photo, as the cleaner had the only other key, so we were back at home but not really, our books and clothes already in the car, people

without baggage. When I expressed my surprise at the X-ray photo, she said that breaking in is much easier than you think, I can do it with a credit card too, and with that encouraging thought I fell asleep. The next morning there was a light mist over the canal, I recognised the cormorant that looked at me with the gaze of wild creatures who do not perceive a human being, and I knew that I had to leave the city and exchange it for the high mountains you always see in the distance from the lagoon when the weather is clear, but I did not want to yet. I stared at the old engravings on the opposite wall, which lately I had seen every morning when getting up, prints from different centuries that wanted to prove that the shape of the city had not changed for a very long time, the voluptuous curve of the Canal Grande, which makes it seem as if the *sestiere* of San Polo by the Rialto wants to bite into the soft belly of the other side, the cemetery island of San Michele across from the Ospedale like a child that wants to swim to its mother, San Giorgio still just a little bit its own fortress at the tip of Giudecca, Giudecca itself with that mysterious rear side that tells the rest of the world that Venice really does stop here. Somewhere in the black tangle of those maps must be the scratched lines of the house in which I was still tucked away, virtually impossible to find when drawn to that scale, an almost physical sensation.

The past few weeks had been good, we had let go of the sense of the city as a duty, had always set off without a plan.

Now I looked at those old maps and understood that the Siberian storm that had held me captive in the city the day before was a message. I did not have to leave at all, I could go to the fish market again, go on another long ride on a vaporetto, and go and look at Arnolde d'Este's magnificent medieval tomb in the Frari one last time. I could extend those past weeks by a few days more, not say farewell for now, and allow myself to drift through the city. The maps on the walls had no colours, I tried to find the place where the Giardini should be now. I had never really thought about those urban gardens, for me it was the place of the Biennale, where I had never been, a green spot on the map where the vaporetto always stopped on its way to the Lido. Now unexpectedly I had the time to look at the peculiar statues that stand there among the bushes, not far from the place where the murdered partisan lies stretched out in the water, her long hair flowing with the seaweed, a memory of a war that I lived through myself. She lies there so still that it is as if the gentle movement of the water is the translation of her thoughts, a meditation on things that disappear behind the wall of time, but for some people always remain present in the secrecy of their hidden essence. Not far from her, there is an entire company of them, if you walk there alone you have the feeling they all know one another, that perhaps you are disturbing them. A man who looks like a heroic Karl Marx with, where his chest should be, something like a gravestone

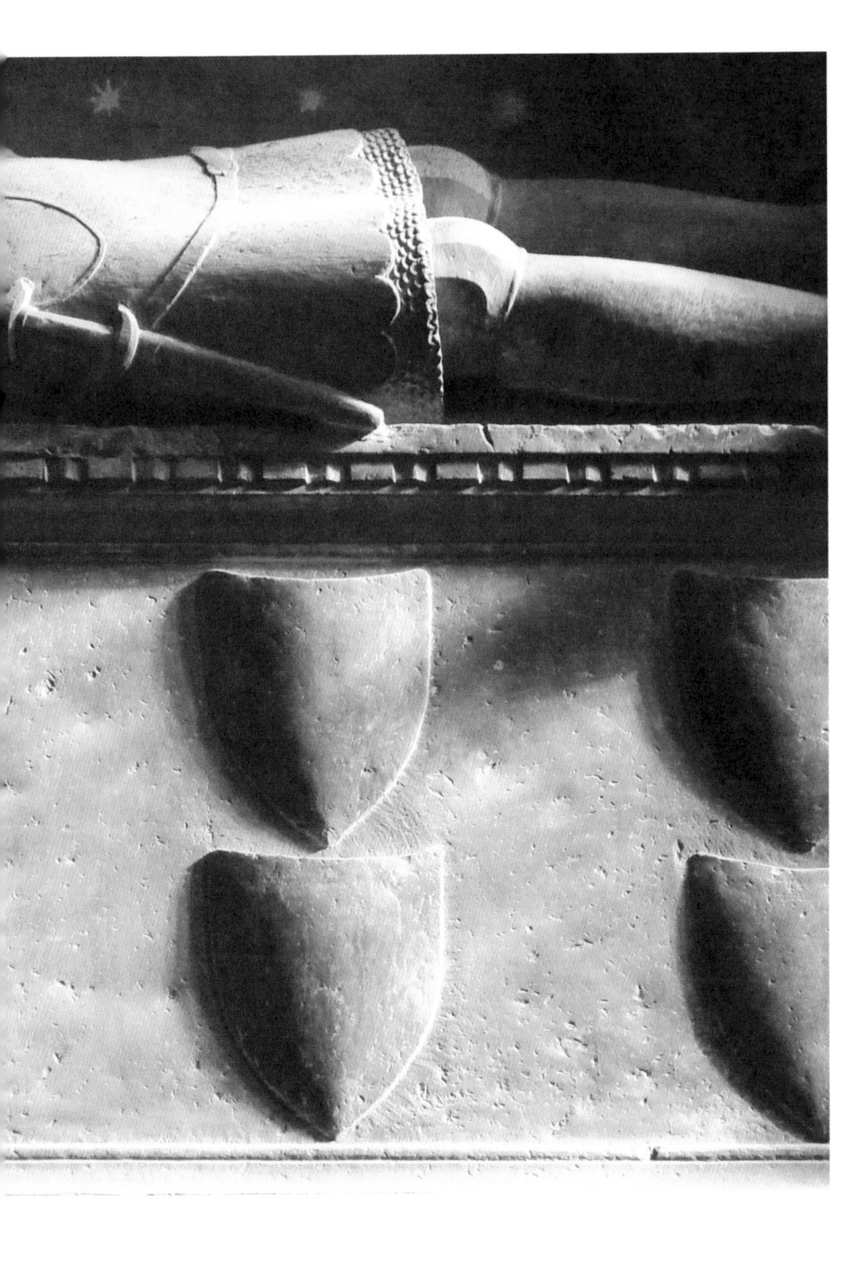

with a name on it, just legible, Giosuè Carducci, and in place of his shoulders two women with their heads turned away from him. He towers high above the branches of bare winter trees, under him a furious black eagle. He was a poet, an Italian who did not believe in God and who won the Nobel Prize in 1906. What do poets think when they see their statues? And what do they think about the company of stone they have joined so many years after their death? Not far from him stands Guglielmo Oberdan, condemned to death in 1882 for attempting to kill the Austrian emperor in Trieste. Hero of Italy, follower of Garibaldi, failed assassination. Italy had lost a large area to Austria, Trieste belonged to the Habsburgs, and it should be returned to Italy. Thirty years later, in Sarajevo, another attack would be carried out on a Habsburger, with the First World War as the result, something of the nationalist passion of those days shines from the blackened face of Oberdan, who was actually called Oberdank, but had sacrificed the "k" of his name before he gave his life. The least Venice could do is remove the black from his dirty face: his head is certainly handsome enough – this is what a hero should look like, collar wide open, chin raised high, jawline firm. Someone has scratched on his chest a circle with an A inside it. Austria? No, Anarchy.

Wandering through a city always means wandering past signs. These statues have all kinds of things to say, Gustavo Modena, Riccardo Selvatico, Pier Luigi Penzo, an actor, a mayor, a heroic pilot with his antique goggles still on his forehead. It is a rainy day, on a park bench an elderly Asian man is sharing his bread with what must be thirty pigeons, I see small birds finding a few bits and pieces to eat on the bare branches of the trees and hear my own footsteps on the gravel of the paths, and I feel good in the company of these statues, it is a friendly cemetery of dead stone people who are standing upright. Wagner, too, who is called Ricardo here, because he died in Venice in 1883, is among them and he looks out over the lagoon, I see from the dates that almost everyone has been dead a century or more, they are used to it, that is probably what makes it so peaceful here. A mutilated Apollo flaying Marsyas the satyr behind a bush and holding a piece of stone skin in his hand, Pallas Athene with her arms in the air on a monumental lion, lost under a laurel tree, I am in the land of dreams on a day I have given myself as a gift, but the best is yet to come, an explorer with dogs, Francesco Querini. Later I read that he was a mountaineer and researcher, who had taken part in an expedition to the North Pole with the Duke of the Abruzzi, and, unlike the duke, did not return from that voyage in 1900. I remember his name now from a trip to Spitsbergen, as they have named an island to the north of Spitsbergen after him. You do not expect to find islands with Italian names in that part of the world, but Querini does not appear too concerned about that now. Somewhere he is resting in the icy arctic cold

without a grave, but here he is sitting high on a rock with his two dogs at his feet – and what dogs they are. They do not want to leave him alone, that much is clear, they are lying against legs, which are wrapped in gaiters up to the knees, and they look at me as if they were expecting me hours ago, but the same is true of their master. All three have a strange, surprised expression as if they have yet to understand how they ended up here in Venice from the polar ice, and I think this is because the sculptor has placed their pupils strangely in the middle of their eyeballs, I can't look away. His name on the monument is worn, if you do not look it up you will never know who he was – he never really came home.

This is all the fault of that mast that fell across the bridge. The empty days I have gifted myself take me to places I have never been before, which lead me to strange thoughts. With my head filled with the statues in the Giardini, I wandered slowly through half the city and, without thinking too hard about it, have ended up in the Museo di Storia Naturale on the Fontego dei Turchi, and I am looking at an enormous gorilla who is hanging on the pale-pink wall with outstretched arms. He is angry, this gorilla, his maw with all those teeth is wide open, on his bare chest is a brass plate saying "gorilla", his feet and hands made of black leather look alike, to his left is the shell of a giant tortoise, what am I doing here?

So many times in this city full of museums with paintings and man-made masterpieces, and now I find myself here, in this museum of things no-one made, among skeletons of prehistoric animals, shelves full of birds that look as if they could still sing, the fossil of a fish from the Cenozoic Era, which looks like a bream I could have bought at the market this morning to poach in white wine tonight.

Wrong, the fish does indeed come from near Verona, where there is no longer any sea, but from 66 million years ago, when Verona and I did not yet exist but this fish did. So it becomes a meditative morning after all. In this city of so many ages, this is also an option, no Tintoretto or Carpaccio today, today in this weird and wonderful museum I am tossed to and fro between eras and extinct species, Venetian

explorers and noble hunters who brought back their triumphs to the city on the lagoon. Venetians had swarmed out once again to discover the world, their spoils are displayed here, and I find myself standing in front of a cabinet that contains two black mummies of crocodiles, alongside the gleaming mummy of a woman, equally black. It is a room dedicated to the Venetian explorer Giovanni Miani. He looks at me from his nineteenth-century portrait with a somewhat melancholy gaze, his broad figure wrapped in what is probably Arab clothing. He had searched for the sources of the Nile between 1859 and 1861, but not found them in time. Some British men succeeded a year later. What he did bring back with him were his lithographs, notes, drawings, his handwritten diaries about the tribes he visited, the things he saw, a treasure trove for ethnologists. Weapons, musical instruments, agricultural tools, all preserved for us in spacious, bright display cases behind those mummies of crocodiles and the black aristocratic skull of the woman lying beside them. Miani believed she was probably a priestess, as described by Herodotus, women who were appointed to feed the sacred crocodiles and who, when the crocodiles died, were promptly killed, mummified and interred together with their animals. When he found her, her face was covered with a golden mask. The crocodiles beside her point forwards, as if wanting to swim past her to some unimaginable future. I try to picture the living woman, the sound of a voice in a forgotten language that is no longer heard by anyone, but the shiny, onyx-like skin of her slender feet and hands makes that impossible, too much time has passed between her and me.

There is an even stranger state of affairs in the peculiar hunting chamber of Count de Reali. This is not a room for animal-rights activists, but it is beautifully done. Death is somehow absent even though dead animals are all around. The endless long necks of giraffes sweep out of their frames on the wall, apes, zebras, heads of deer with elaborate antlers, stuffed snakes standing upright, their forked tongues pointing threateningly at me, tiger and lion skins on the floor and on the wall, ivory tusks, another long neck, this time an ostrich, directly opposite the gorilla, truncated elephant legs as tables, an absurd and hilarious panorama whose wonderful symmetry makes it seem a little like a tribute to the insane multiplicity that nature has dreamed up for itself, an evolutionary cabinet of rarities. Somewhere in a corner hangs the oil painting of the count who collected and most likely killed all this, a somewhat balding gentleman in a tie, under a thick layer of varnish, with bulging eyes that still appear to be aiming, and whose horizontal moustache, extending far beyond his cheeks, makes him resemble one of his curious victims. When he died, the family donated this entire treasure to the city. Past the skeleton of the *Ouranosaurus nigeriensis*, terrifying even now at three metres tall and seven metres long, I walk back into the Venetian afternoon and see a gull on the quay by the water, hacking with its violent beak into what is left of a pigeon before tossing it into the water. When I get home I see my cormorant taking a long dive into the grey water, and resurfacing after a while some distance away. How many millions of years before he is permitted to be in a museum?

Even before my failed departure I had bought not only two books by Donna Leon in a beautiful bookshop, both of which had to do with the lagoon, but also a small and exquisitely designed book by an Italian author I did not know, Rosella Mamoli Zorzi. Italian names are cantilenas, perhaps that is why Italians are so fascinated by northern authors, something about those names, so grinding for a southern tongue, seems to contain secrets that the southern soul wants to seek out. The opposite happens to me, I hum Mamoli Zorzi, Rosella to myself in reverse order, and have already purchased the book, partly because Veronese's *The Rape of Europa* is on the cover. The thoughtful head of the decorated bull that will abduct her, Europa's blonde, plaited hair, the fate awaiting her, the milky-white throat with the small necklace, the one, virginal breast, just as white, among that profusion of fabric and jewels, the swirling movements of all those female bodies in their abundance of textiles, this little book is irresistible. It is called *Wonder and Irony* and it describes the emotions and thoughts of Henry James and Mark Twain when looking at the work of Tintoretto and Veronese in the Doge's Palace.

In my sudden free time, everything seems possible again. It will not be the first time that reading a book has changed my day. I had visited the Doge's Palace and the Basilica frequently in the past, but generally avoided them in recent years because of the large crowds and the long queues, while at the same time feeling guilty about it. It has started to rain, I have been sitting in a café, looking at and reading the book, two Americans could not be more different. James, highly intelligent, a well-read aesthete, in what he writes he resembles the portraits I know of him, a reflective man who was very good at looking, not only at paintings, but also at his fellow Americans abroad, the protagonists of his books. Rosella Zorzi has found the right passages in those books, *Italian Hours, The Princess Casamassima, The Golden Bowl, The Wings of the Dove*, everywhere he sees – or the characters in his novels see – paintings, they talk, write and think about them, in *The American* he even has his protagonist buy a painting, which will become the cornerstone of a collection, in short, James, slowly and gracefully, moves through a painted universe, it is the end of the nineteenth century, he must have had the time and leisure in the Doge's Palace to contemplate the Veroneses and Tintorettos in peace, and even though he knew when to stay away from other tourists, they were tourists of a different kind, people more like himself, he lived in a different era, not disturbed by disobedient school classes and inconceivable Chinese people with inconceivable selfies, and was able to incorporate what he had seen into his books, an upper-class American, who had come by boat because aeroplanes did not yet exist and who walked around in the past power and wealth of Venice with an enviable self-assurance and at the pace of a sea voyage. I picture fine shoes, polished by someone else, a three-piece suit, a gold watch chain, a past that is gone for good, in which he did not have to doubt anything. Does he see the same paintings as I do? I have come from the outside deck of a vaporetto, got an unpleasant soaking on the Schiavoni, and now I stand in a long queue of damp contemporaries held in check by a tight rope, every so many minutes a group is allowed in, when we are finally inside we try to dispose of our wet clothes in the cloakroom. As always, we get lost in the enormous dimensions of the mighty building, it is pouring down upon the large open courtyard, we wander, chilled through, up and down the stairs and galleries, Henry James is nowhere to be seen, in every room there is a board with an explanation and a jumble of people crowding around, I pretend to have no body and read about what I am seeing over the shoulders and past the ears and ridiculous headgear of other people, the inhabitants of the realm of Ovid, heroes and mythical creatures, gods and goddesses, *The Rape of Europa*, about which James wrote to his famous brother, the philosopher William James, that "it is impossible to look at it without aching with envy" as "nowhere else in art is such a temperament revealed" as here in "the mixture of flowers and gems and brocade", the writer, who is not yet thirty, goes into raptures about it, in his story "Travelling Companions" he ecstatically continues with lyrical descriptions of Veronese's *Rape*, such as, "I steeped myself with unprotesting joy in the gorgeous glow and salubrity of that radiant scene, wherein, against her bosky screen of immortal verdure, the rosy-footed, pearl-circled, nymph-flattered victim of a divine delusion rustles her lustrous satin against the ambrosial hide of bovine Jove." I look again, and no, I am not going to doubt his high-flown prose with my later eyes, such things make no sense, I see the nymph's right leg only just touching the "ambrosial hide" of the divine bull. Jupiter was abducting the beautiful Europa, he looks deep in thought, his bull's head inclined, like an old man tolerating the tumult of the women's bodies on and around him, and I think of the same scene in a painting by Nikolaas Verkolje in the Rijksmuseum, about which I once wrote long ago, and then I see, because the people in front of it have suddenly left, in another corner of the Sala dell'Anticollegio the small painting by Tintoretto that James also writes about, *Bacchus and Ariadne Crowned by Venus.* After the gigantic walls of Tintoretto's *Paradiso* in the Sala del Maggior Consiglio, this small painting is a marvel of simplicity. In his story "Travelling Companions", James returns to the difference between the two paintings and the two painters in a conversation between two of his characters, how can the sombre painter from the Scuola San Rocco also have made this light, enchanting painting, "this dazzling idyll"? And he is right, when I later look at other paintings by Tintoretto in other places in the palace, the mystery only increases. Venus seems to be flying as she places the crown on the head of the seated Ariadne, the slender Bacchus keeps the two female figures in perfect balance, the left hands of the two women touch under the gloriously bright sky, it is a dream of a painting.

How long ago did Henry James stand here? A few wars

ago is a correct answer and therefore an abyss to ponder in the palace that has itself waged so many wars and amassed so much wealth that I can still look at that very same painting today, the Venetians have preserved their treasures well. Just for a moment, time is cancelled out; just for a moment, I am Henry James and everyone who has seen this painting in the past five hundred years, and in the midst of all those people around me I once again have that peculiar sensation for a second, the feeling that I have no body, and I wander on through the large galleries until Mark Twain awakens me abruptly from these dreams with an ironic task, and that is the "Irony" in the title of the book. Henry James was the "Wonder", signifying enchantment and amazement at the same time, while Mark Twain, the writer of *A Tramp Abroad*, can bring me back to earth with a sentence that I only understand when I have finally found the object he is talking about, a tramp, a wanderer, after all, has a different way of looking at things.

The painting in question is by Francesco and Leandro Bassano and is to be found in the Chamber of the Council of Ten, but if you are imagining a picture, then you will stand, stunned, at the entrance to the room for a moment, as this is an endless painting from wall to wall. The first thing you see is a pope who is apparently blessing a doge with the appropriate gesture, and a doge who is not kneeling for that blessing and then, further to the right, after a large group of men with banners, the enormous rump of a battle horse, a grey that takes up more room than the Pope and the doge put together – but that is not what Mark Twain saw. I have his words with me, and I can read English, but still I do not understand what he means when he gives the Bassano painting a different name. "The other great work which fascinated me was Bassano's immortal Hair Trunk." From that point on, my self-appointed task was to find this immortal Hair Trunk among the huge number of people on the wall. Dogs, horses, men with lances, mitred bishops, a pope, a doge, a woman with a child, a man bending over to two dogs, and my eyes have covered only a few metres, I am still nowhere near Pope Alexander III, who is giving his blessing to Doge Sebastiano Ziani under a canopy that is raised aloft. Later I look up Ziani in my book of doges. He was the thirty-ninth doge, and reigned from 1172 to 1178. He was not only the man who founded the first state bank, but he also brought about the reconciliation between Alexander III and Emperor Frederick Barbarossa, the famous story of the kiss and the stirrup just in front of San Marco. The wealth of Venice, already inconceivable at the time, certainly helped. At the end of his life, Ziani retreated to the other side of the water and the monastery of San Giorgio Maggiore. Things here are not only close in space, but you can hear echoes in time too, when you think that this same doge ensured that the emperor also signed a truce with the Lombard League, the Lega

Lombarda, a name that still reverberates in this century in the Lega Nord – in this place history is never far away.

But where is my Hair Trunk? For Mark Twain, this mysterious object must have been the centre, perhaps even the protagonist, amidst the hustle and bustle on the wall. To the right of the Pope and the doge stand the high and mighty with flags waving, further along I see soldiers, a drummer, a man who is leaning over the wheel and the barrel of a cannon, then the enormous horse I mentioned earlier and which only now I notice is accompanied by another grey, with a black man wedged in between as a contrast to these two white horses. Still further to the right someone is blowing a trumpet, and then the Hair Trunk "bursts with an electrifying suddenness on the spectator, in all its matchless perfection". "From that moment," writes Twain, "no other thing in those forty feet of canvas has any charm; one sees the Hair Trunk, and the Hair Trunk only – and to see it is to worship it." I would like to do exactly that, but I do not really see what he means, and I am not alone, as Twain continues, "Bassano even placed objects in the immediate vicinity of the Supreme Feature whose pretended purpose was to divert attention from it yet a little longer and thus delay and augment the surprise." As far as I am concerned, it has worked because still I cannot see it, which is of course the intention: you do not see it until you see it, and then you know that you have been fooled by a master storyteller. Behind the horse's monumental backside, a jagged halberd lies on the ground, and behind that there stands a man with a heavy sack on his back, barefoot and followed by another man in blue and, yes, I think what enormous pleasure the painter must have taken in painting such a diverse crowd, and finally I see it, still in fact hidden under the barrel of a cannon: a small, hairy trunk, the thing that, according to Twain, this whole enormous painting is about. The fact that another man comes after, and the high stern of a galleon, with beyond a sky of an indescribable blue, beneath which a number of ships lie at anchor, is no longer relevant. I try to look as closely as I can at the small trunk, gleaming brass nails have been hammered through the fur, in the darkness of the room the protagonist is almost invisible, Twain has succeeded, I have forgotten pope and doge, all I would like to know now is what art historians think of this, and if Henry James ever read the story of his fellow American writer, who was so different from him. Rosella Zorzi says nothing about this, and I wander on through the mighty building. Through a window in one of the corridors I see that it has not yet stopped raining, I hear the sound of a ship's horn in the distance, I reflect on the fact that the monastery of San Giorgio, which still exists, is just a vaporetto stop away, the place to which Doge Ziani retreated eight hundred years ago, not knowing that three hundred years later he would have to surrender his place of honour next to the Pope to a fur-clad trunk, on the later orders of an author from a continent that, at the time he was ruling, had not yet been discovered by the West.

Prezzo a richiesta! Price on request! FOR SALE!! So it says on the cover of the magazine of the *Corriere della Sera* of February 22, which I have kept. An illuminated cloud hangs over the Canal Grande, evening mood, a gondolier rows an empty gondola across the grey water, you see the lights from the street cafés, façades, vaporetti in the distance, and read the big white letters of the title, VENDIAMO VENEZIA? Are we selling Venice? Everything must go?

La Serenissima, the most serene one, is the literal translation of the epithet that has been attached to Venice for centuries. But is it still correct?

Inside the magazine, a big picture, one of those cunning photographs with which you can shrink or magnify a city, distorting the perspective, so that nothing is right anymore. Usually you do this to prove something, and that is the case here. Front left is a narrow moat, which is the Canal Grande, with across the water Santa Maria della Salute, a large building on a small body of water. The picture is all wrong, but the church is clearly recognisable. What is much more recognisable, however, is the enormous cruise ship behind it, which the editing has made appear larger than half a city, you could put five Salutes next to or in front of it. Beyond the ship, a wide stretch of water, after all we are still in La Serenissima, but in the grey sky above is written in large letters "*Noi Veneziani? Non stiamo serenissimi!!*" – "We Venetians? We are not *serenissimi!!*" The author of the story is Tiziano Scarpa, but with my imperfect Italian he immediately puts me on the wrong track, since he is having a conversation with someone (I think) who lives below him. *La riconosco*, I recognise her, he says, *è una pantegana* (and I did not know that word) *grossa*, a big rat, a giant sewer rat who lives beneath me.

Tiziano Scarpa is the author of novels and of a subtle book about Venice, and he gets that Venetian rat to say: "There is one thing we Venetians cannot do. We cannot hide. We have no metro, no options for escape underground, we live on the surface, we live without a subconscious, Venice is built on mud, its inhabitants are the most superficial people in the world, we have no nooks to which we can flee to preserve our identity. Other cities have catacombs, bunkers, we have no underground anti-tourist shelters to protect us from the aerial onslaught of low-cost tourism."

As an Amsterdammer, you understand at once, even though we do have a metro. In the article you read about everything you have seen happening in recent years, but now with figures. There are only 55,000 Venetians left, in a city visited by 30 million tourists every year. Venice has, in fact, already been more than sold. Within the area of San

Marco, 90 per cent of the restaurants are run by Chinese, Albanians and people from the Middle East. What follows is a plea. The income Venice generates is huge. In the publicity material that lures tourists to Italy, Venice, with its history, its incredible art treasures and its Biennale, is one of the major attractions. The money from all those millions of tourists does not only stay in the city but also goes to Rome. Can the Italian State not at least do something in return to protect the city? From the dangers of the water, from decay?

The mafia, the 'Ndrangheta, are already there, the extreme bureaucracy persists. You only have to read a couple of thrillers by Donna Leon to know what is going on. Recent history, the battle against the ever-increasing rise of the high water, fraught with corruption and scandal, is a dramatic example. The writer cites a gondolier. How once upon a time they did not merely transport people who wanted to sit ignorantly in a gondola for half an hour, but also those who really knew something about the city, who asked to be taken to particular churches, people who were there for their love of the city, scholars, a better kind of tourist. I know the stories about the other tourists, and I also know the strategies Venetians have come up with to deny the plague, to ignore it. I know the action that has been taken against the big ships, the silent and the not-so-silent resistance. In these ice-cold weeks of February and March, the great flood has ebbed away a little, Venetians do not have to contend with the foreigners who have taken their usual seat at their favourite café, and as I am writing this I am aware that I too am a tourist, that I can leave before the summer and the great hordes arrive, and of course everything you say about it has two sides, and then another two sides, but if you have been coming here for so many years you can imagine the sentiments only too well, the big sale, the feeling that others are slowly but surely taking possession of your birthright, of what you believed was inalienably yours for ever, people who do not speak your language, who walk over your memories, who do not know the secrets from which every city is constructed for its inhabitants, those things you cannot explain or communicate, unless that foreigner, by means of what he or she has written or done, has become part of the city's history, as in the cases of Montaigne, Byron, or Casanova once upon a time, and later Henry James and Ezra Pound or Peggy Guggenheim, Thomas Mann, Ernest Hemingway and Mary McCarthy, names that have taken on the colour of the city because the people attached to those names had lived here or written about this place.

Last Day

A LAST DAY, OR WHAT SEEMS LIKE IT. WHERE DO I SAY farewell? Morning coffee with the *Gazzettino* at a café on Piazza Santa Margherita. For the last time I disguise myself as a Venetian, attempt to order something without an accent, want to stay hidden, mimicry, sit in the dim sunlight by the window, a man with a newspaper, look at the fish stall where I will not buy fish today. When will I return? Since that first visit, in 1964, I have been travelling around the world for more than fifty years, but I have always come back, a special form of homesickness. And yet I have never chosen to live here, perhaps because all my life I have felt as if I have never truly lived anywhere. But then what is it that makes you love this place more than other places? I try to think about it and get no further than the word peculiar, in the sense of special, one of a kind. This city is incomparable, its history, people, buildings, but it is not the individual buildings, events, characters, it is the totality, the accumulation of very big and very small things. It is the city itself, it is the people who have

made her, this absurd combination of power, money, genius and great art. First they claimed their city from the lagoon, then they drifted out across the great oceans beyond, returning again and again to the city that was their home, always protected by the wise, wide water, often so still and yet sometimes so dangerous, that has enclosed her on every side until in this century, with rising sea levels, it became a greater danger than ever before, and as I think about all of that I know I want to spend this day on the water, but I do not want to go to Murano or Torcello, I want to go to the island I do not yet know, Sant'Erasmo, the vegetable garden of Venice. This island plays a special role in the last book I read by Donna Leon, *Earthly Remains.* I will not go into the details of the thriller, as I am interested in just one aspect right now, the depiction of two men rowing on the infinity of that water, men who know the waterways. When I read the book, I took out the extensive map of the lagoon, waterways in water, which is what fascinated me about that map. One man is older than the other. He has retreated to that small island, and since his wife's death he has lived there alone. Here and there in the lagoon, he has beehives that he visits. Sometimes they are far away, and that distance is described. The man who is rowing with him is Commissario Brunetti, the protagonist of Leon's novels. Brunetti is younger than the other man, whose name is Davide Casati. He has come to the island to rest. Something clicks between the two of them, a long, long time ago Davide won a regatta with Brunetti's father, and that creates a bond. And of course Davide rows better than the city-dweller Brunetti, who soon realises that his body cannot really keep up on that first day, that he is getting blisters on his hands. The rowing of the two men is captured beautifully. We do not know at that point that the older man will die at the end of the book, a death that has to do with what is perhaps the most important theme of all of Leon's books: the corruption in and of Venice, running rampant over everything, construction, real estate, adoption, permits, restaurants, smuggling, art. But that first day is not about corruption, it is about the open water, the silence, the birds. As I am writing this, I have the map in front of me. I know where they were rowing to on that first day, on the map I see canale San Felice, but "canal" gives the wrong impression. Water is, as on every map, coloured light blue. But what does it mean when, amidst that light blue, the words Canale di San Felice are written in fine letters between extremely thin lines in a darker blue? Are those lines shores? No, not really, they are waterways in the water, and then you see it, side canals, very subtle erratic curves, indications of marshland, sedge, reed beds, land just under water, for anyone who loves names there is one delight after another: Motta dei Cunicci, Ossario di Sant'Ariano, and further away the Palude Maggiore, which the early Venetians, first pursued by the Ostrogoths, later by the Lombards, left to flee to the muddy islands that would become their city.

The Davide in the story knows where he can sail, where he can moor, there is a silence between the two men that is accompanied by the splashing of the oars, as I read it I could hear that silence, I felt the younger man slowly breaking into the silence of the older man, everything they hear and see creates a remarkable sense of calm. I know that vaporetto number 13 leaves Fondamente Nove for Sant'Erasmo every hour. There are not many passengers, we stop once at Vignola, where it is busy in the summer because the city dwellers flee there when it is hot. Two people get off, a girl and a man who has a bicycle waiting for him, with a touch of jealousy I watch them disappearing into the landscape, curious about their lives. As we sail away, it seems as if the world is opening up, and yet it is only a short journey. I think I can see Burano in the distance, the boat stops at Capannone on Sant'Erasmo, and the movement of the few people on the boat leads me to think this is where I should disembark. I do not ask any questions but wait to see what will happen. In Donna Leon's book, this is where Brunetti gets off and meets Davide Casati. I see a few people coming to the stop, they are neither tourists nor city folk. Sant'Erasmo is not large, but it is long, these are people who know one another, they have rustic faces, with the sea and the wind written upon them. I can see from their looks that they register the strangers that we are, or simply take note of us. There are only five of us now. I had decided to get off at the Sant'Erasmo

Chiesa stop, as I thought there would probably be a café by the church, but there is nothing. We are the only ones who get off, the others are going to the only stop there is after that. The boat leaves, and for some time I can still hear the sound of the engine. Close to the church there is a column with, perched up high, a bird with outspread wings. The silence is overpowering, so the letters on the column are all that speak. They talk about honour, about heroism, Sant'Erasmo will not forget those who sacrificed their tender years on the altar of the fatherland. I do not know if I have understood it correctly, but there is something about a vermilion flower, a flower perfumed with human virtue. All that eloquence is confusing, and there are no names. The church is low, small, intimate. The doors are open, but there is no sign of anyone. Beside the high doors, just two narrow windows, so the church looks like a fortress – the lagoon can get rough. The top of the façade looks like a cloud, successive waves of white. Inside, a mosaic with a crowned Christ and his mother, their Byzantine feet in small tiles angled on a small platform, with Saint Erasmus kneeling beside them. When I go back outside, I still cannot see anyone. I have taken a leaflet from the church, an Arabian legend about a sultan. I recognise the story, it is the Gardener and Death, familiar from the famous poem by Van Eyck that ends with those unforgettable lines, as Death expresses his surprise that "This morn at work I see here the man I am to fetch tonight from Isfahan." The next story is about a Zen master. Japan, Persia, I am far away, and yet I have disembarked into the middle of the global world. When a small pick-up drives past later, it is an event. At random we stroll first some way to the left, and then to the right. A vineyard, houses in the distance, the occasional parked bicycle, far away the sound of a tractor, a small harbour, boats without people, mooring posts, grey mists, low land in the distance, almost Dutch. I think of the rowing trips Leon describes in her book. Their boat passes between sedge and reeds, the sand used by the glassblowers of Murano over the centuries shimmers through the shallow water. There, too, the silence is perfect. The two men sail, their little boat is a *puparín*, a forerunner of the gondola, and Commissario Brunetti has his eyes wide open. "Brunetti had rowed since he was a boy, but he knew he had little to contribute to the smoothness of this passage. There was not the least suggestion of stop and go, of a point where the thrust of the oar changed force: it was a single forward motion, like a bird soaring on rising draughts of air, or a pair of skis descending a slope. They reached the end of the island and turned eastward, following the shoreline past houses and abandoned fields. [...] He turned, then, to watch Casati row. Seeing the perfect balance of his motion, back and forth, back and forth, hands effortlessly in control of the oar, Brunetti thought that no man his own age or younger would be able to row like this because he would spoil it by showing off. The drops from the blade hit the water almost invisibly before the oar dipped in and moved towards the back. His father had rowed like this."

All I want now is to see a boat on the water, the rowers outlined against the light of the horizon, but the only thing there is to see is the water itself, a grey, gleaming expanse in which only a few people know the secret ways, we walk along the narrow road between the green fields and the water, Venice is far away yet close, and as I walk there to the beat of my steps, with the wind as a companion, I try to think about the wonder of all this, a city built by people in this water, a species of human that dreamed an insane dream in this watery landscape, in my mind I see a city of palaces and churches rise above the water, such a vision as never seen before. Once upon a time, the Venetians fetched the relics of Saint Mark the Evangelist from Alexandria and made his leonine aspect the symbol of their city.

No-one has painted that lion more beautifully than Carpaccio with, in the distance on the left, the Doge's Palace and on the right a number of ships with billowing sails. Left in the foreground, bushes, a tree, a piece of land almost invisibly merging with the water to which the city was married, and in the middle of all this the lion with the transparent circle of his halo around that angry, imperious head, and behind his maned neck the long wings stretched out, suddenly making him into a bird as well. Mighty and lithe, he stands

firm on the ground but also dominates the water and the air above, master of all the elements, come to Europe from antiquity, his right leg with the paw and sharp claws lying powerfully upon the upright book. The two pages at which the book is open are gleaming white, the words on that shining page cannot be missed: *Pax tibi, Marce, evangelista meus,* peace be unto you, Mark, my evangelist. Myths can do anything, they can make a Jewish follower of a crucified teacher write a book that will continue to exist through the centuries, they can give wings to the lion that belongs with that man, and the power to protect a city, they can place that lion high on a pillar on the piazza of that city, from where he can look out over the lagoon, and there he stands: a lion above the city and the water.

September 2018
Sant Lluís

Acknowledgements

Lines from the following works are reproduced with thanks:

Joseph Brodsky, *Watermark* (London: Penguin Books, 1992/New York: Farrar, Straus & Giroux Inc., 1993)

Alejo Carpentier, *Concierto Barroco*, © Alejo Carpentier, 1974, and Heirs of Fundación Alejo Carpentier, 2018

Michael Dibdin, *Dead Lagoon* (London: Faber and Faber, 1994/New York: Pantheon, 1995)

Valeria Luiselli, *Sidewalks*, Translated from Spanish by Christina MacSweeney (London: Granta Books, 2015/Minneapolis: Coffee House Press, 2014)

Illustrations

All photographs are by Simone Sassen, reproduced by permission

The Tempest by Giorgione, from the Gallerie dell'Accademia di Venezia, © Photo Scala, Florence

Venice, Rialto Bridge from the South by Canaletto, reproduced by permission of the Gallerie Nazionali di Arte Antica, MIBACT – Bibliotheca Hertziana, Istituto Max Planck for the History of Art/Enrico Fontolan

The Annunciation by Tintoretto, reproduced by permission of the Scuola Grande di San Rocco, Venice, © Scuola Grande di San Rocco

Bibliography

J. L. Borges, "El jardin de senderos que se bifurcan", *Ficciones* (Buenos Aires: Editorial Sur, 1944)

Joseph Brodsky, *Collected Poems in English* (Oxford: Oxford Poets, 2001)

Joseph Brodsky, *Less Than One* (London: Penguin Books, 1986)

Alejo Carpentier, *Concierto barroco* (Madrid: Alianza Editorial, 2012)

Jorge Carrión, *El libro de los pasajes* (Barcelona: Galaxia Gutenberg, 2017)

Giacomo Chevalier de Seingalt Casanova, *The Story of My Life* (London: Penguin Classics, 2001)

D. S. Chambers, *The Imperial Age of Venice, 1380–1580* (London: Thames & Hudson, 1970)

Louis Couperus, *Uit blanke steden onder blauwe lucht* (Amsterdam: L. J. Veen, 1912)

Carlo Favero & Giorgia Favero, *The Discalced Carmelites in Venice*, Translated from Italian by Jeremy James Scott (Cittadella: Biblos Edizioni, 2015)

Federico Fellini & Bernardino Zapponi, *Le* Casanova *de Fellini, Scénario* (Paris: Éditions Albin Michel, 1977)

Amable de Fournoux, *La Venise des Doges* (Paris: Éditions Tallandier, 2012)

Marina Gasparini Lagrange, *Labirinto veneziano* (Barcelona: Candaya, 2010)

Donna Leon, *Earthly Remains* (London: Penguin Random House/Arrow Books, 2017)

Donna Leon, *Through a Glass Darkly* (London: Penguin Random House/Arrow Books, 2007)

Giulio Lorenzetti, *Venezia e il suo estuario* (Rome: Istituto Poligrafico dello Stato, 1956)

Rosella Mamoli Zorzi, *Wonder and Irony with Henry James and Mark Twain in the Venice Ducal Palace* (Venice: Supernova Edizioni srl, 2018)

Predrag Matvejević, *Das andere Venedig* (Klagenfurt: Wieser Verlag, 2007)

Mary McCarthy, *Venice Observed* (New York: A Harvest Book, 1963)

Eugenio Montale, *Collected Poems 1920–1954*, Translated and annotated by Jonathan Galassi (New York: Farrar, Straus & Giroux Inc., 1998)

Eugenio Montale, *Selected Poems* (Harmondsworth: Penguin Books, 1969)

Paul Morand, *Venetiës*, privédomein nr. 136 (Amsterdam: De Arbeiderspers, 1988) and *Venices*, translated from French by Euan Cameron (London: Pushkin Press, 2013)

Lothar Müller, *Casanovas Venedig, Ein Reiselesebuch von Lothar Müller* (Berlin: Klaus Wagenbach, 2009)

John Julius Norwich, *A History of Venice* (London: Penguin Books, 2003)

Rev. Alexander Robertson, *Fra Paolo Sarpi, the Greatest of the Venetians* (London: Sampson Low, Marston & Company, 1894)
Andrea di Robilant, *Venetian Navigators* (London: Faber & Faber, 2011)
Giandomenico Romanelli, *Venedig, Kunst und Architektur*, 2 vols (Cologne: Könemann, 1997)
John Ruskin, *The Stones of Venice*, edited by J. G. Links (Boston: Da Capo Press, 2003)
Tiziano Scarpa, *Venice is a Fish*, Translated from Italian by Shaun Whiteside (London: Serpent's Tail, 2008)
Toni Sepeda, *Brunetti's Venice: Walks through the Novels* (London: William Heinemann, 2008/New York: Grove Press, 2009)
Salvatore Settis, *Wenn Venedig stirbt* (Berlin: Klaus Wagenbach, 2015)
Philippe Sollers, *Casanova l'admirable* (Paris: Gallimard, 2000)
Miklós Szentkuthy, *Marginalia on Casanova, St Orpheus Breviary*, Vol. I (New York: Contra Mundum Press, 2012)
Hippolyte Taine, "Venise", from *Voyage en Italie* (1866) (Paris: Éditions Grand Caractère, 2006)
Gary Wills, *Venice: Lion City* (New York: Simon & Schuster, 2001)

CEES NOOTEBOOM was born in 1933 in The Hague. His first novel, *Philip and the Others*, appeared in 1955, and since then he has built up an impressive oeuvre of novels, poetry, short stories and travelogues. His work has earned him numerous awards, among which the Bordewijk Prize and the (American) Pegasus Prize for *Rituals* (1980), and the Aristeion European Prize for Literature for *The Following Story* (1991). The latter was translated into more than twenty languages and signalled his international breakthrough. In 2004 he was awarded the prestigious P. C. Hooft Prize for his entire oeuvre. Among his other books are the novels *In the Dutch Mountains* (1984), *All Souls' Day* (1998) and *Lost Paradise* (2004). His travelogues include *Roads to Santiago* (1992) and *Roads to Berlin* (2009), which won him the German 3rd of October Literature Prize. Together with his wife, the photographer Simone Sassen, he has also made an illustrated work *Tumbas*, on the graves of writers, philosophers and poets. He lives between Amsterdam, the island of Menorca (the inspiration for his book of non-fiction, *Letters to Poseidon*), and southern Germany.

LAURA WATKINSON has lived in England, Scotland, Italy and Germany. In 2003, she settled in the Netherlands. Her previous translations include Cees Nooteboom's *Roads to Berlin* and *Letters to Poseidon*, Peter Terrin's *Post Mortem*, Otto de Kat's *The Longest Night*, and Tonke Dragt's *The Letter for the King*.